INSECURITY AND SUCCESS
IN ORGANIZATIONAL LIFE

INSECURITY AND SUCCESS IN ORGANIZATIONAL LIFE

Sources of Personal Motivation Among Leaders and Managers

David L. Rothberg

PRAEGER SPECIAL STUDIES • PRAEGER SCIENTIFIC

Library of Congress Cataloging in Publication Data

Rothberg, David L.
    Insecurity and success in organizational
life.

    Bibliography: p.
    Includes indexes.
    1. Leadership. 2. Control (Psychology)
3. Executives—Psychology.   I. Title.
BF637.L4R67   658.4'09   81-11881
ISBN 0-03-059854-0   AACR2

Published in 1981 by Praeger Publishers
CBS Educational and Professional Publishing
A Division of CBS, Inc.
521 Fifth Avenue, New York, NY 10175 USA

©1981 by Praeger Publishers
All rights reserved
123456789 145 987654321
Printed in the United States of America

TO LUCIAN PYE,
TEACHER AND FRIEND

PREFACE

In this study of the psychology of leadership among 330 business and military elites, we seek a better understanding of what drives organizational leaders to pursue power and success. Are influential leaders driven by some nagging feeling of personal insecurity? Does their pursuit of power represent an attempt at reconciling discordant needs and drives, or allaying a disturbing conflict that exists between personal goals and professional expectations? Is the need for control of other men compensatory in nature, or does the pursuit of power have its basis in the "healthy" personality? If the latter be the case, we may ask, Do people who seek positions of prominence do so because they sincerely believe they can improve their organization and effectively achieve its goals?

Traditionally, bureaucracies have been viewed as a haven for lazy and inefficient managers. The dynamic leader, many have presumed, willfully shuns bureaucratic organization because of the constraints it would impose upon one's imagination and urge to get things done. Weber, Merton, and dozens of other scholars of organizational behavior have viewed bureaucracies as a stultifying, if not powerful organizational vehicle by which behavior is routinized for ritualistic rather than goal-directed ends. Unique personal qualities, more often than not, are swallowed up by behavioral proscriptions attached to group norms.

Canonized in William Whyte's famous work *The Organization Man,* the typical bureaucrat has been portrayed as a strangely anxious blend of ambition and deference. While he vigorously pursued success, he rarely took risks. For the way to get ahead was to please one's superiors and remain "well liked" even if not well respected. In this study we focus not only on the classic "organization man" but also on the "self-starter." That is, the continuously motivated leader who takes initiatives and exposes himself to risk by bending and even breaking the rules of bureaucracy for the sake of organizational (or personal) gain. Like Whyte's organization man, the self-starter is an ideal type. Properly speaking, there is some self-starter and some organization man in all who inhabit large organizations. One of the goals of this book, therefore, is to see the degree to which the ideal type of self-starter is present in different kinds of leaders and managers.

In this presentation of each of four leadership types—rational, existential, administrative, and entrepreneurial men—we ask ourselves: "In what ways, and why, does this leader take initiatives and attempt to change his organization? What are the motivational forces that underly the activistic impulse, and what is the personal meaning of his initiative-taking behavior? If he is a true self-starter, why is he so? Is he driven by some subjective feeling of inadequacy as Lasswell and Weber have suggested, or does he take initiatives as a natural manifestation of his need to express himself and as a way to improve his job and his organization?

In Chapters 1 and 2 we introduce the reader to the participants in the study, lay out the research design, and raise the issue of whether varieties of insecurity or anxiety serve as drive mechanisms or psychological preconditions for the taking of unsolicited initiatives. Also, we present the leadership typology that serves as the foundation for this work. The typology is based on the interactive effects of insecurity and the subjective perception of the degree to which leaders believe they have control of both their own actions and the activity that takes place in their environments. In these introductory chapters we show how leadership is intimately bound up with character and world view.

In Chapter 3 we present the first leadership type, the "rational man." An organizational leader who experiences both high self-esteem and strong feelings of control, the rational man is much the utilitarian. He has a strong need for achievement, he is persuasive in his dealings with others, he is comfortable with his high status, and he takes initiatives only when they will result in instrumental gain. The classic utility maximizer, the rational man's pursuit of success is premeditated, well planned, and well defined. Because this type of leader is not anxiously driven to act by any insecurities or deep-seated needs for power or control, the rational man is probably the least interesting of the four types. Yet, paradoxically, the rational man does not always fare well as a "reality tester." For the rational man believes his capacity to control his environment is so complete that he is oftentimes unrealistic and apt to overestimate his leadership capabilities.

While the rational man views the world and the manifold problems with which he is faced as reducible to comprehension through rational activity, the second leadership type, the existential man, experiences a world composed of irrational social forces. Because the existential man does not think all problems have solutions, his behavior is not (as it is for the rational man) "rational" or highly analytic in nature. Rather, the existential man is intuitive, visceral. He acts to change his environment even in situations where he has incomplete information, or even when he is disturbed by uncertainty. Psychodynamically, the rational man and the existential man offer a qualitative contrast in world views and in per-sonality. They are psychologically different. The preoccupation with activity in the face of uncertainty is the essential paradox of existential man and the subject of Chapter 4.

In Chapter 5 we introduce the administrative man, a manager whose struggle centers around his perception of how he is viewed by other people in the organization. It is not so much production, per se, or the solving of difficult problems that causes the administrative man to be anxious. Rather, it is how others will receive and evaluate what he produces that causes anxiety. The administrative man is deeply concerned about whether or not his behavior is considered conformist by his colleagues. The point of uncertainty is not, as it is for the existential man, where the forces of the world impinge upon the goals of the individual, but it is where the individual's capabilities and sense of compromise collide with the world's expectations. The administrative man is interesting because his professional accomplishments derive from a basic sense of insecurity, yet his actions often result in the betterment of the organization.

In Chapter 6 we not only fill out the typology by presenting the character, world view, and leadership style of the fourth type of leader, the entrepreneur, but we take the opportunity to test a very controversial theory about the nature of man. In this chapter we seek to ascertain whether those corporate and military elites, whose characterological structure mirrors that of Max Weber's famous entrepreneur, indeed act as did Weber's entrepreneur. That is, we seek to investigate whether the powerful leader who is both inhibited and lacking in subjective fate control seeks to resolve his insecurities through ascetic and purposive activity aimed at the accumulation of organizational currency (that is, power). In Chapter 6 we also attempt to find out how the meaning of seeking or accepting a challenge actually renders unimportant the success or failure of the challenge outcome.

In the final chapter of this work we discuss the complex relationships that exist between personality and the attainment of success in corporate and military organization. We then identify and systematize the distinguishing psychological characteristics that differentiate leaders from managers.

Placed into three analytic formulas that derive from Lasswell's famous explanation of political man, our a priori model of leaders and managers is borne out by showing how leaders are both promoted more rapidly and come to acquire more visible positions of power than managers.

ACKNOWLEDGMENTS

Many of the ideas expressed in the following pages come out of six years of lively and entertaining discussion with Lucian Pye. As both a friend and a teacher, it was Lucian who asked many of the provocative questions that led to the undertaking of this book. His generosity and unremitting concern are warmly appreciated.

I am also deeply indebted to Lloyd Etheredge and Ithiel de Sola Pool. Lloyd has been an ongoing source of support, stimulation, and encouragement. I have benefited greatly from his many readings of this work and from many conversations we have had about the psychology of people in power. Ithiel's interpretation of Max Weber has helped immeasurably, and his sensitivity to the problems of doing empirical research has caused me to search for many an alternative explanation.

I would also like to thank Ruth Lane, Glynn Wood, and Jim Kirkman for contributing to the development of my early thinking about the psychology of elites and power. I would like to thank Herbert Hyman for his comments on the initial research design and David Winter and Henry Brady for reading the early drafts of the manuscript and providing many useful suggestions about how to present the data. I am also grateful to David Winter and McBur and Company for allowing me to use the comparative TAT data that I present in Chapters 3 and 5 and to Robyn Baris-Steinhilber for assisting me with the content analysis presented in Appendix IV.

Chris Argyris, Chuck Gibson, Phil Orso, Claudyne Wilder, and Jim Short also read all or parts of the manuscript, and their interpretations and suggestions are appreciated.

Finally, I am indebted to Chuck Gibson and the Harvard University Graduate School of Business Administration and Franklin Margiotta of the Air Command and Staff College for assisting in the collection of my data and to Eugene Skolnokoff and Amy Leiss and the Center for International Studies at MIT for helping to support the research that made this book possible.

CONTENTS

LIST OF TABLES

LIST OF FIGURES

INSECURITY AND SUCCESS IN ORGANIZATIONAL LIFE

CHAPTER 1

CLASSIFYING POLITICAL MAN

Why is it that some men are marked by qualities that make them worthy of leadership and others by qualities that destine them forever to be followers? In trying to answer this keynote question, thinkers have been led to classify men, attributing to them some ideal or distinctive characteristic that distinguishes them from the common man. Few have been so vivid as Plato (Lane, 1973: 1), or more prosaic:

> Citizens, we shall say to them in our tale, you are brothers, yet God has framed you differently. Some of you have the power of command, and in the composition of these he has mingled gold, wherefore also they have the greatest honor; others he has made of silver, to be auxiliaries; others again who are to be husbandmen and craftsmen he has composed of brass and iron . . . and God proclaims as a first principle to the rulers, and above all else, that there is nothing that they should so anxiously guard, or of which they are to be such good guardians, as of the purity of the race . . . for an oracle says that when a man of brass or iron guards the state, it will be destroyed.

Following Plato, some powerful and picturesque classifications focusing on leadership types have been developed. During the Renaissance, Machiavelli (1971) envisioned a world inhabited by lions and foxes whose cunning and prowess enabled them to rise above (if not wile their way around) the common man. During the late 19th and 20th centuries, Pareto (1935) sought to classify powerholders or elites, and while he was hesitant to animate his types of leaders with the instincts of the lion or the fox, his typology was remarkably similar to that of Machiavelli: Pareto maintained that the ruling elite governed by "cunning" or "force" (Bottomore, 1964).

While the types of men described by Plato are cast of gold, silver, or iron and brass, modern thinkers have been less ready to cast their types of men in such pure or solid forms. Ignoring the wisdom of the oracle, modern social scientists no longer ask the same guiding or keynote question. The nature of our inquiry has changed, our level of ignorance reflected in perhaps the more appropriate and current question that guides our work: "What *is* leadership?" Is it a unique personality characteristic as the ancients have suggested, a structurally determined role, or a special combination of personality, opportunity, and fate?

There is at present little agreement on whether leadership is any or all of the above. While psychologists have often viewed leadership as a personality variable, sociologists have viewed leadership as somehow structurally determined. Political scientists, depending on their persuasion, have viewed it as either one or the other, or some combination of both, steering a safe and perhaps reasonable middle ground. As the debate continues, it is becoming more and more apparent that further research will not yield a ready set of answers to the problems raised in posing the current question. Nevertheless, through the years many thinkers have analyzed the "leader" and considered his acts of leadership (and the style by which he exercises his "power") as deriving from "personality."

Since Lasswell's (1930) famous trichotomy of agitators, administrators, and theorists, a series of attempts at understanding not only the behavior exhibited by different types of political leaders, but their private sources of motivation as well, have been generated. In a more or less empirical vein, Spranger (1966), Barber (1972), Maccoby (1976), and others have sought to distinguish types of leaders not only by examining salient patterns of behavior but also the psychological preconditions thought to actuate that behavior. McClelland (1961, 1976) has sought to understand a special type of modern man, the "entrepreneur," much as did Schumpeter (1962) and Weber (1958) before him.

Man is a complex animal living in a complex world. Leadership as a phenomenon reflects this complexity, and one way in which leadership may be analyzed is to simplify its variegated forms. Typology building, which seeks to embrace a whole range of disparate behaviors in a systematic and organized fashion, is an appropriate tool of analysis. Max Weber, in his *Methodology for the Social Sciences* (1949:137), succinctly described the power of the typology, an analytic tool at least as old as Plato:

> The construction of abstract ideal types recommends itself not as an end but as a *means*. (The ideal-type) is a conceptual construct (Gedankenbild) which is neither historical reality nor even "true" reality . . . It has the significance of a purely ideal *limiting* concept with which the real situation or action is *compared* and surveyed for the explication of certain of its significant components. Such concepts are constructs in terms of which

we formulate relationships by the application of the category of objective possibility. By means of this category, the adequacy of our imagination, oriented and disciplined by reality, is judged (Weber's italics).

LEADERSHIP AND POWER IN BUREAUCRACIES

The present study is a direct examination of the needs, drives, and private motivations of an American business and military elite. Shaped in the typological tradition, it will focus on leadership style through examination of more than 330 de facto powerholders. The typology with which the reader will be presented has been designed not only as a socio-psychological classificatory schema but as a vehicle by which a series of leadership behaviors and general traits of style may be explicated and understood.

"Organization Man" and the "Self-Starter" in Bureaucracies

Many bureaucratic leaders are effective norm enforcers, "organization men" who nimbly execute organizational directives and established policy. An inertia of habituation characterizes their leadership style. A select few, however, are deft at initiating directives and policy and in so doing, perhaps even create norms.

Of central concern to us is the leader who takes initiatives. The "self-starter," as we shall call such a leader, is a self-directed and continuously motivated man who takes initiative for the betterment of his organization. Not coincidentally, some self-starters may take initiatives for the betterment of themselves—to acquire more prestige, to enlarge their domain of power, or even to compensate for some real or perceived inadequacy. It is evident that both the organization man and the self-starter are needed by the organization because both serve important functions. The designations "organization man" and "self-starter" are, of course, ideal types or pure forms, but they are surely more fluid than Plato's men of gold, silver, or brass and iron. There is some self-starter and some organization man in every bureaucratic elite.

The organization man and the self-starter are different kinds of leaders, marked by qualitatively different characteristics. While the self-starter *acts* on impulse from within, the organization man *reacts* to imperatives framed outside himself—imperatives, or perhaps force of habit, generated by the norms of his organization and his own role expectations.

But what makes the self-starter "tick"? Does the self-starter as differentiated from the average bureaucratic leader take initiatives because he is comfortable with his place in the organizational hierarchy, confident of his abilities, and supported by superiors and subordinates alike? Is he a man who is psychologically "free" from the anxieties tied to leadership, unbridled to act on his creative impulses? Or does the self-starter, much like Weber's entrepreneurial man, take initiative, seek to have impact, and attempt to bring about organizational change because of some insecurities he may be harboring—insecurities that may cause him to act? Is it possible that the self-starter is driven to act on his environment out of fear that it will act on him, and with negative consequences? Could it be (as Lasswell suggests) that a personal sense of insecurity or anxiety, a sense of weakness, could provide the psychological impetus for taking forms of action that could be of benefit to the organization (personal benefits accruing to the self-starter not withstanding)? Does the self-starter, the man who takes initiative, the leader who strays from the normative path laid before him by his organization, take risks that the organization man avoids, even fears? Can we equate such risk taking with attempts at innovation? Throughout this work, attempts will be made to answer these and related questions about leadership personality and behavior in complex organizations.

Traditionally, bureaucracies have been criticized as being the natural habitat of people who wish to avoid risks and are fearful of taking initiatives. Equally uncomplimentary has been the popular view that those who are the most successful in climbing bureaucratic ladders are usually overly ambitious, power-conscious people who are primarily concerned with their own interests. Psychologically oriented research about people in bureaucracies has tended to parallel these layman views, often dwelling on the presumed "crippling" effects of success in hierarchical organizations. What has not been adequately studied is why some leaders are motivated to take initiatives and expend their efforts for creative purposes. What are the psychological characteristics of such motivated people? How do they differ from those who are less successful and less prepared to be activists? Before answering these questions and developing both the typology and the theory of the self-starter, let us briefly look at the leaders who are the subjects of this study.

STUDY PARTICIPANTS

The sample of leaders who have been analyzed for this work are recent graduates of a midcareer executive program at the Harvard Business School and midcareer air force officers currently attending the Air War College and the Air Command and Staff College. Within the framework of our basic concern with identifying the characteristics and motivations of the activist organizational leader, comparisons between business and military groups will be made. The study as a whole, however, will not be a general descriptive comparison of the two groups.

The rigorous screening procedures employed by these two instititutions, coupled with corporate business and Pentagon appointment procedures, allow us to predict that a large proportion of executives and officers attending these institutions will very shortly join the American business and military elite. Many are already elites.[1]

The Corporate Executives

The business executives who participated in this study were enrolled in the midcareer Program for Management Development at Harvard University during 1977. At the time data were collected they had a mean age of about 37. About 97 percent are men, and most are married. About 28 percent of these executives have an M.A. or a Ph.D. in their field(s) of specialization, and they have worked professionally for about 12 years. On the average, they have worked in more than three separate positions in their sponsoring organizations and earn a salary well over three times the national average. Some of the older participants earn well over $100,000 per year.

In total, 31.5 percent of the executives are one level away from the chief executive officer position in their companies, 31.2 percent are two levels away, and about 20 percent are three levels away. The average number of subordinates reporting to the typical program participant is 171, while for a handful it is greater than 1,000. These elites represent over 39 industries, with large numbers coming from banking, the chemical, electronic machine, and oil industries, and other concerns whose decisions greatly affect the everyday lives of the mass public (see Table 1.1). Follow up data on past program members clearly indicate that participants have been carefully preselected by sponsoring organizations and will attain some of the most powerful positions possible in their respective industries. Many are already vice-presidents and general managers for multinational conglomerates.

A Military Elite

A study of military elites in transition by Margiotta (1979) has shown that a major compositional shift has taken place within the last two decades. During all but the last few years in U.S. history, military elites have come largely from rural southern backgrounds and have had less formal education than other elite segments of society. Within the last two

Table 1.1: The Business Elite

Type of Industry		Position Within Industry	N
utilities	petroleum	Assistant General Manager	(9)
construction	government	President	(1)
manufacturing	electronics	Director/General Manager	(36)
banking	computers	Vice-President	(20)
chemicals	transportation	Staff	(1)
foods	steel/metals	Treasurer	(2)
insurance	land development	Supervisor	(1)
aerospace	engineering	Administrative Officer	(1)
retail trade			
		N =	71

decades, however, the composition of the officer class has changed, so much so that a majority of the military leaders are now coming from the northern industrial states. Concurrently, a strong emphasis has been placed by the military on technical and educational skills, and therefore many officers now have advanced degrees (65 percent as compared with 28 percent for the business population). The social and psychological implications of such a shift are multiple and affect not only intramilitary relations but also relations between the military and society at large. Table 1.2 presents a rank and management compositional breakdown of the military elite who participated in this study.

These officers are rigorously selected out of a much larger pool of career officers. Only 16 to 22 percent of all major selectees attend intermediate schools (such as the Air Command and Staff College) and only between 12 and 18 percent of those selected for lieutenant colonel attend senior schools (such as the Air War College). On-time colonel promotees (or colonels who have not been promoted in an accelerated

Table 1.2: The Military Elite

Rank	Institution	Management Level	N
Major	Air Command and Staff College	Mid-level Management	(155)
Lt. Colonel	Air War College	Upper-mid-level Management	(76)
Colonel	Air War College	Executive-level Management	(29)
		N =	260

fashion) do not attend senior service schools (Margiotta, 1979:17). The military sample, then, is composed of proven midcareer elite officers. Many, especially among colonels and lieutenant colonels, will move into decision-making capacities in the Pentagon.

Empirical data have been derived from samples of two divergent elite populations because the following analysis seeks to describe types of elite self-starters and their leadership style. This study thus will be largely limited to intra-elite comparisons. However, a number of measures that have been used in the survey research instrument, which all respondents have completed, have been widely tested with nonelite groups. Comparative reference will therefore be made to nonelite groups where baseline data are available.

Within the elite sample we will identify the self-starters both by psychological measurement and by career advancement records. Among the Air Force officers we have records of those who are "above the zone" (that is, promoted ahead of their peer class), "in the zone" (promoted with their peers), and "below the zone" (those promoted more slowly than the majority of their peers). These official promotional classifications will be referred to throughout the work.

THE IMPORTANCE OF PSYCHOLOGY IN EXPLAINING ELITE BEHAVIOR

Possibly the dominant school in administrative theory has been the one that stresses structural imperatives and communications patterns in decision making and problem solving (for example, Barnard, 1938; Blau, 1974). While some scholars of this school have sought to minimize, if not completely deny, the importance of personality, most have recognized in varying degrees that personality can be an important and at times decisive factor in administrative behavior. Herbert Simon, in the preface to *Administrative Behavior* (1957), states that "the central concern of administrative theory is with the boundary between the rational and the non-rational aspects of human social behavior." Similarly, Amitai Etzioni (1975), in his classic study *A Comparative Analysis of Complex Organizations*, states that elites differ according to the "source of their power" (which may be derived from the actual organizational office), their personal characteristics, or both.

A second major school in the mainstream of administrative theory attempts to apply the findings and methods of social psychology to organizational behavior. Katz and Kahn (1966) deal primarily with human relations within organizations, but they also treat the problem of leadership, which is the concern of this work. Their typology of leadership styles, much like that of Downs (1967), revolves around types of strategies and cognitive skills employed by leaders, but to the extent that they treat affective considerations it is largely in the context of interpersonal relationships and not basic human motivations.

A third tradition that this study utilizes is that of the "elite theorists." This is a tradition that has been strongly sociological in that attention has been drawn to the background or demographic characteristics of elites. It is true that one of the earliest elite theorists, Gaetana Mosca (1939), did try to identify the distinctive inner quality of elite classes, but he could say little more than that the individuals of which these classes were composed had greater "vigor" and "drive" than the common man. Similarly, Pareto (1935) attempted to identify an elite model personality, but as Carl Friedrich (1950) has said, Pareto failed "to show that 'elites' as defined by him possess a distinctive group characteristic." Indeed, in general, it can be said that this sociological tradition has acknowledged the importance of psychological variables, but as Bottomore (1964: 51-52) has commented:

> little or no attempt is made to establish by exact methods of investigation that the . . . kinds of personality which are alleged to determine the characteristics of . . . elites actually exist, or to describe them precisely in psychological terms, or to show that there are not other varieties of political personality.

Although the present study relates in varying degrees to these essentially structural, sociopsychological, and sociological elite traditions, it is above all a study of the disparate motivations and world views experienced by successful elites. As such, it belongs to a long and theoretically strong tradition. In a sense, this study begins, as did David McClelland in his classic study *The Achieving Society,* with Max Weber, who uniquely combined an interest in psychological motivation and the nature of modern bureaucratic organizations. Our analysis of the motivational basis of leadership behavior is very much influenced by David McClelland himself and the pioneering work of Harold Lasswell, which we feel has not been adequately followed up with rigorous testing and systematic revisions.[2]

The importance of individual psychology in explaining elite behavior in complex organizations has been acknowledged by proponents of all traditions of organizational behavior analysis. As has already been noted, both the structuralists Simon and Etzioni emphasize the critical place of personality. Janowitz (1960: 41), after a detailed analysis of military organization (which may be called sociological in nature), admits to the impressive fact that only 1 percent of American pilots accounted for 30 to

40 percent of all enemy planes shot down in World War II—thus identically trained men in standardized organizations and with equal opportunities had tremendously different rates of performance, which can only be explained by variations in "personality." Similarly, with respect to business organizations, Rensis Likert (Tedeschi, 1974: 291), after reviewing 25 studies conducted by the Institute of Social Research, has concluded that the "most effective managers and supervisors are using procedures and practices which differ in important ways from those advocated by their companies"; that is to say, success is not apparently correlated with adherence to standardized norms but with individual, personal qualities.

Various contemporary theorists have sought to identify the key characteristics of the psychological dynamics of successful managers and leaders. Argyris (1959) suggests (in the spirit of Lasswell's classic formulation about political man) that successful executives "use" the organization for their personal needs (just as the organization "uses" the individual executive for its needs), and that the most salient personality factors seem to be "self-control," "powermindedness," "problem-solving mindedness," and "self-motivation." Choosing among a series of important personality factors, McGregor selected self-control as being the most important for leadership (Bennis and Schein, 1966), but, again, he did not seek to describe this variable in any rigorous psychological depth. In a recently published book, McClelland (1976) gave theoretical impetus to the study of organizational leadership and a theory of motivation, though no aggregate data have been collected to test his most recently formulated hypotheses.[3]

The analysis presented here begins with an understanding of the organizational leader as a person whose motivations mirror those of Weber's economic (or "entrepreneurial") man and Lasswell's political man (or "homo politicus"). It views the highly motivated leader as an individual characterized by different combinations of self-esteem, insecurity, and fate control. Yet other psychological and structural variables are important and will be discussed so that we may present an analysis not only of different types of activist leaders but of other kinds of leaders as well (such as the more passive "administrative man").

PSYCHOLOGICAL ISSUES

The first objective of this study has been to develop a typology of organizational leadership personalities. The typology, as indicated, will be based on a series of important psychological qualities that have been measured and utilized in many studies in the past.

Self-Esteem and Insecurity—How Do They Affect Leadership?

Max Weber, in his classic *The Protestant Ethic and the Spirit of Capitalism*, noted that the successful entrepreneur seemed to have a strange blend of wanting to be of the elect but having considerable anxieties as to whether he was. Weber believed that the combination of some elements of self-assurance and some degree of insecurity was a powerful motivating force. Since Weber's insights, social psychologists have refined many concepts that seem to get at the phenomenon Weber was describing. In part, Weber was concerned with one's estimation of self-worth, as perceived through earthly activity. We now call this estimation self-esteem, though of course, self-esteem can entail much more than self-evaluation.

A person's level of self-esteem affects one's willingness to undertake new and challenging tasks as well as the manner in which one behaves when interacting with others. Self-esteem has been viewed as a stable personality dimension, though in a real sense, it is a process that can continuously evolve over time and change as we experience success and failure.

Persons with high self-esteem differ from those who are low in self-esteem in their reactions to situations that are relevant to the satisfaction of their personal and professional needs. Individuals experiencing strong feelings of self-esteem can be expected to react to new situations with expectations of success, since characteristically they have been successful in the past. Those with low self-esteem often approach new situations with the expectation that they will in some way fail. Researchers (for example, Hovland and Janis, 1959) have shown that persons high in self-esteem both attempt to exert more influence than persons of low self-esteem and are less susceptible to being influenced.

Like all measures that the present study shall report, the measure of self-esteem is contained within a questionnaire that all respondents were asked to complete.[4] This particular measure consists of a ten-question scale that has been "normalized" so that respondents may score between 0 and 100. Throughout the work, judgments concerning the respondents' levels of self-esteem will be made with regard to their relative score on this index.

Belief in the Ability to Control One's Fate—
How Does It Affect Leadership?

"Internal-external locus of control" refers to the extent to which persons perceive "contingency relationships" between their actions and their outcomes (Rotter, 1966). People who believe that they have some control over their destinies are called "internals," while "externals" believe their fate is attributable to extrinsic forces or agents such as luck, chance or some other unknown.

It should be noted immediately that those who believe that they themselves control their own destinies may be either high or low in self-esteem. To believe that one is the master of one's fate is not the same as being self confident. (As we will illustrate in Chapter 5, certain kinds of leaders feel they are in control of their fate, yet they remain highly insecure.) Similarly, people who believe they are not in control of their fate (externals) may be either high or low in self-esteem. These people may feel very positive about themselves because of other personal capabilities, their experience of incomplete control notwithstanding.[5]

A great portion of the fate-control literature has shown that while internals are highly active and goal-directed, externals are often emotional and incapable of focusing on specific goals. Yet this study will show that high organizational status may be obtained by both rational and emotional types of leaders. Goal-directed instrumental traits of style characterize only one of many operative strategies available to the successful organizational elite.

The organizational leaders who participated in this study answered Julian Rotter's (1966) complete 29-question internal-external locus of control battery, which measured the extent to which they felt they controlled or were controlled by other people, themselves, and their work environment. When throughout this work reference is made to a leader's perception of control, evidence will be based on the summated score of these 29 questions.[6]

In Chapter 2 we will discuss the interaction of self-esteem and fate control and present a typology of organizational leaders based on this interaction and on the kinds of leadership behavior it produces.

NOTES

1. It was of great import to analyze the social-psychological processes that have impelled these chosen few into positions of power while they were amenable to systematic investigation. Social scientists cannot readily administer psychological tests and detailed questionnaires to people who are powerful and busy leaders. Indeed, because of the relative inaccessibility of high status leaders, previous studies of the behavioral configurations of elites have generally had to rely on secondary psychobiographical data, descriptive cross-national data, and other essentially demographic information. The sample upon which this study is based represents the nearest potential elite we have been able to identify from whom we can also gather hard psychological data. The War College and the executive program at Harvard are for us convenient stopping points that bring together many leaders whose disparate and often unrelated career paths would never cross.

2. The explanatory power of Lasswell's theory was derived from the psychoanalytic tradition. This mode of observation does not readily lend itself to testing through analysis of mass data. The present study utilizes mass data on leadership personalities and, in so doing, does indicate that there is a conceptual meeting ground for these two distinct traditions of inquiry.

3. In Chapters 4 to 6 we will explore some of McClelland's major hypotheses concerning "combinational motive systems" and organizational leadership.

4. See Methodological Appendix VI.

5. For the business and military elite who participated in this study, a moderately strong inverse relationship was found between self-esteem and locus of control ($r = -.28$, $p < .001$); yet the relationship between locus of control and self-esteem varies widely between business and military groups (treated separately) and among the four types of leaders.

6. The reader is referred to Appendix II for an explanation of how the 29-question fate-control construct was scored.

CHAPTER 2

THE LEADERSHIP TYPOLOGY

Thus far we have outlined the meanings of self-esteem and fate control and have briefly indicated how these two very powerful personality dimensions can affect the behavior of leaders. What we must now be concerned with is the interactive effects of self-esteem and fate control and the personality types that their juxtaposition suggests.

Intuitively, and with considerable evidence, it may be argued that it is only when one has feelings of personal efficacy that an individual will seek to change his environment, communicate freely with his peers, participate in organizational decision making, and seek to be a leader. Coupled with the belief that one is able to control his destiny, the individual with a strong sense of self-worth would believe his actions will *make a difference*. But attempts at becoming successful may not always originate in the active personality driven by high self-esteem and the ever-present belief in the ability to control one's fate (see, for example, the many writings of Harold Lasswell). The pursuit of elitehood may be the manifestation of doubts about the ability to achieve continued success. Lasswell (1930) has shown how such doubts or a general sense of insecurity may gain prepotency over all other personality needs and drives, creating anxiety-ridden, yet "effective" leaders.

In the present study we will typologize the active elite personality as one of high self-esteem or one of low self-esteem, in combination with a subjective perception of control—that is, whether one believes he controls his fate or whether one believes he is controlled by it. This typology delineates four faces, or minds of power (see Table 2.1). The first face of power is certain both of his ability to achieve and of the fact that his destiny resides within (he is found in quadrant I of the typology); the second face of power is certain of his ability to achieve, yet at the same time is unable to

Table 2.1:   The Leadership Typology*

	Fate Control	
	Internal Locus of Control	External Locus of Control

High Self-Esteem	I. *"Rational Man"*
	
	Persuasive
	High need for achievement
	Resistant to influence
	Trusting
	Efficacious
	A "utility maximizer"
	Comfortable with his
	  high status
	As a "reality-tester"—
	  fair
		II. *"Existential Man"*
		
		Seeks to manipulate
		Decisive
		Places high value on the
		  concept of "time"
		Dominant
		Persuasive
		Has a "command identity"
		Bold risk-taker
		Uses interpersonal
		  influence tactics
		Seeks control

Insecurity	III. *"Administrative Man"*
	
	Very high need for
	  achievement
	Strong need for approval
	Strong "hope of power"
	Strong need for affilia-
	  tion
	Sustains norms
	Displays reformist
	  sentiments
	Takes organization's
	  goals as own
	Strong sense of responsi-
	  bility
		IV. *"Entrepreneurial Man"*
		
		Inhibited
		Seeks personal confirmation
		Goal-directed
		Mistrustful
		Highly uncertain
		Strong sense of duty
		Self-improving
		Needs recognition
		Successfully completes,
		  but does not enjoy
		  tasks
		Is alienated from the
		  orgnanization

*See Appendix I for operational definitions of the four types.

claim mastery over his fate (quadrant II); the third face of power, while convinced his destiny lies in his own hands, harbors doubts concerning his ability to make that destiny a desirable one (quadrant III); and the fourth face of power represents the man who is both uncertain of his fate and his ability to achieve continued success. The critical point of convergence for the four ideal types lies in their common active posture toward their environment.

The operational strategy of this study will be to examine how a particular cognitive configuration or internal state of mind (as schematized in the typology) provides a type-specific view of the world that in turn predicts leadership styles and general traits of action—particularly the taking of initiatives for creative purposes within large organizations:

CHARACTER → WORLDVIEW → LEADERSHIP STYLE

FOUR TYPES OF LEADERS

Rational Man

Quadrant I of the typology contains those leaders we have called rational men. This type of leader is active and certain—the self-assured, persuasive person who is a high need achiever and is generally resistant to outside influence. Much akin to the classic utilitarian, the rational man experiences an ordered and predictable world. As the "rational" world is understandable, rational men seek control through highly analytic, achievement-oriented activity. Always a utilitarian, this type of leader prefers calculation to impulsiveness.[1]

The psychological freedom enjoyed by our rational man allows him to act on his creative impulses. But his acquisition of formal organizational power evolves not from a love (or a need) for working on challenges. Rather, this type of leader achieves success because the successful accomplishment of challenges gratifies him and provides him with tangible rewards.

While the rational man is no less, and perhaps even more, a capable worker and leader than the organizational leaders schematized in quadrants II and III, he is less likely to conform to our model of the self-starter, for he experiences no discomfort concerning his ability to achieve continued success or his capacity to control his professional fate. He is both active and certain; he is goal-directed, comfortable with his high status and success, happy in his work, and feels quite content with his proven "formula" for success. An expectancy of succeeding characterizes and drives this man's leadership style.

Existential Man

It has been generally recognized since the writings of Harold Lasswell that people who actively pursue elite status are likely to be anxiety-driven and have feelings of inadequacy that dominate but do not inhibit their other personality needs and drives. Thus, it is to quadrants II, III and IV that we naturally look to find leaders who are also likely to be self-starters. These may be the gifted few who take immediate command in the absence of outside stimulus, who seek information through subtleties in their environment, and who are perpetually self-actuating. As active leaders, perhaps they are somehow able to block out the inhibiting affects of anxiety, fear, and doubt surrounding decision, though they are, of course, profoundly anxious and in need of reassurances.

In the case of individuals falling in the second quadrant, ambiguity concerning the ability to control one's fate drives the leader with high self-esteem into continuously acting on his environment—to secure both his organizational responsibilities and his self-esteem. He is flexible, opportunistic, and decisive. Paradoxically, he is an emotional, highly ego-involved man. As he is uncertain about his ability to control the world, time is of essence. While he is decidedly active, he is uncertain—not about his proven ability to achieve but about his ability to control. This sense of uncertainty drives the existential man and encourages a leadership style that makes use of interpersonal power tactics. More than any of the other leadership types, the existential man assumes a "command identity." At the same time, he expresses very little inhibition. Seeking to be "in the right place at the right time," the ambiguity that this type of leader experiences concerns not his ability to produce, but his capacity to control individuals and work outcomes in the organizational milieu. That he is uncertain of his fate but is high in self-esteem makes for an interesting paradox.

Administrative Man

While the leader schematized in quadrant II is unable to reconcile the uncertainties he experiences in his environment, the active self-starter schematized in quadrant III is driven by an uncertainty concerning his inherent ability to achieve. He very much believes in himself as an achiever, yet constantly struggles with his propensity to produce. While he is quite competent in occupational problem solving he feels little comfort when having to deal with people. While he expresses an inordinately strong need to achieve, these expressions are, in part, derived from a lack of confidence when facing others. Because the administrative man experiences anxiety when dealing with others, he tries very hard to relate to others in a positive manner. His handling of power often becomes very emotional, inhibiting decisive, detached strategems for getting ahead. The administrative man is thus the most affiliation-oriented of all the leadership types, seeking the approval of others and not power over them. This type of man is well suited for leadership in large organizations—he is psychologically equipped for enforcing rather than creating normative courses of action.

Entrepreneurial Man

While individuals falling in quadrant II are driven by ambiguity or uncertainty concerning their ability to control, and individuals falling in quadrant III are driven by experiential anxiety concerning their ability to achieve, people who fall in quadrant IV experience more complex (and perhaps more interesting) feelings concerning both their ability to achieve and their capacity to control.

Both locus of control theory and research in the area of self-esteem would predict that individuals who are both insecure and uncertain of their fate would be unfit for leadership in organizations (Coleman et al., 1966; MacDonald, 1973; Wylie, 1961; Lefcourt, 1976). More often than not they would fall prey to their affects, become non-goal-directed, deferential or hostile, mistrustful, anomic or withdrawn. Certainly they would be ill equipped as leaders of men in an organizational context that adheres to a sharply defined ethos.

Yet the data presented in Chapter 6 clearly show this need not be the case. Entrepreneurial men as a group have significantly less control than our whole business and military elite as well as the general population at large. And, as a group, they are significantly more insecure than either our rational or existential men or the whole business and military populations. Yet, within this group of people are fourteen lieutenant colonels, two full colonels, five directors or general managers of large corporations, one president, one vice-president, and a host of other luminaries.[2]

The cognitive configuration of these people has clearly not prevented them from attaining formal positions of power, yet it has strongly affected the ways in which their power has been accumulated and expressed.

Although most Americans today are preoccupied with finding "meaning" in their lives and in their work, the entrepreneur completes the task with which he is faced not out of any special intrinsic love of his work but because he feels it has to be done. He seeks confirmation, is constantly testing, and is ever in doubt about proving his self-worth. As Weber (1958) has argued, the entrepreneur is an inhibited man who attempts to control his impulses through self-discipline.

Unlike the rational man, the entrepreneurial man does not take initiatives in order to maximize his self-interest. Unlike the existential man he does not take initiatives as a manifestation of his need to control others. And unlike the administrative man, he does not take initiatives in order to receive the approval of others. Entrepreneurial man takes initiatives in order to validate or prove his sense of worth. And, not coincidentally, he is a capable worker. And why shouldn't he be—the entrepreneur is the embodiment of the Protestant ethic.

WEBER AND MODERN PSYCHOLOGY AT THE CROSSROADS

Our fourth type of leader, entrepreneurial man, exhibits a cluster of personality and leadership style attributes that accentuate the tensions inherent in the two schools of thought that have most influenced this work. On one hand, and largely utilizing a neopsychoanalytic approach, we have the work of Max Weber and Harold Lasswell. Both these great social scientists believed that leadership was inextricably bound up with, indeed caused by, varieties of personal insecurity.[3] Lasswell's homo politicus acted to compensate for perceived feelings of inadequacy, and Weber's entrepreneur pursued innovation and wealth as the surest means of proving self-worth and eradicating doubt. Both Weber and Lasswell viewed leadership as essentially compensatory in nature.

In contrast to the tradition of Weber and Lasswell stands what may loosely be called modern-day psychology. It views the leader and the innovator as essentially free from insecurity. Insecurity or anxiety, while not viewed as aberrant, is seen as somehow militating against or interfering with the creative impulse and leadership effectiveness. Both personality theory and social-psychology strongly suggest that insecure individuals are unfit for positions of leadership. Such individuals are more likely to be alienated or merely disinterested.

The dialogue between the Lasswell-Weber school and modern psychology goes something like this:

Weber: The genesis of the entrepreneur's anxiety is his doubt about whether he can affect (that is, control) his future. This concern with control creates a unique motivational state that provides for the (secular) "spirit" of capitalism. Anxiety, we may conclude, creates the psychological foundation for the activist, acquisitive impulse.

Modern-day psychology: The individual who believes in luck, fate, chance, or other exogenous forces to the exclusion of "personal causation" (as does Weber's famous God-fearing entrepreneur) is one who is likely to experience a lack of accord between his intentions and his desired outcomes. This incongruity, we may safely say, brings anxiety. Anxiety, we may conclude, causes social quietism, ineffectiveness, and oftentimes, withdrawal.

The two traditions thus agree that the man who believes he lacks control of his fate is a man who is insecure. The point at which the two traditions diverge concerns the effects of this insecurity.

Figure 2.1 illustrates the presumed effects of personal insecurity and

Figure 2.1: The Effects of Insecurity: Weber and Modern Social-Psychology

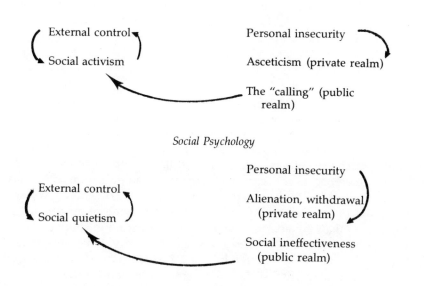

Weber's Man

External control
Social activism

Personal insecurity
Asceticism (private realm)
The "calling" (public realm)

Social Psychology

External control
Social quietism

Personal insecurity
Alienation, withdrawal (private realm)
Social ineffectiveness (public realm)

the perception of external control as posited by the two schools of thought. While Weber's entrepreneur and Lasswell's homo politicus act in the public interest to allay private anxieties, social-psychology envisions the insecure man as self-defeated and socially quietistic. The dialogue of the two schools thus raises two distinct questions: (1) Is insecurity the "cause" of, or somehow bound up with, leadership? (2) Does the experience of exogenous control produce an activistic or quietistic orientation toward the world?

Implicit in our presentation of the fourth leadership type is a test of the Weber thesis. In this test we will attempt to ascertain which of the two schools is more correct. But for now, the reader is asked to examine what follows as against this theoretical dissensus.

THE MEANING OF ANXIETY IN THIS STUDY

Anxiety has been viewed by many as one of man's most compelling drives. Yet anxiety as a concept is vague and hard to pin down. Because it has yet to be adequately defined, it is not surprising that it cannot easily be identified and measured. Harry Stack Sullivan (1953:11) has said that "anybody and everybody devotes much of his lifetime, and a great deal of his energy ... to avoiding more anxiety than he already has, and, if possible, to getting rid of some of the anxiety." Sullivan, Horney (1939), and others believe that anxiety is the cause of many kinds of behavior. Similarly, Presthus (1962:104) has remarked: "The internalization of approved values creates a built-in capacity for anxiety as the desires of the individual collide with society's expectations."

We all often feel, in a very unspecific and fuzzy way, uneasy or uncomfortable when we lack adequate control of situations that are important to us (or perhaps even situations that are unimportant to us). For example, many of us have experienced the uneasiness associated with being lost while driving on unfamiliar roads. A compulsive or neurotic anxiety is obviously of different magnitude and kind from the commonplace anxiety that results from lack of control. In the present work when we make reference to anxiety or uncertainty resulting from either incomplete control or doubts surrounding the ability to achieve, we are referring not to any necessarily neurotic anxiety, though it may be more deeply rooted than the anxiety that arises when lost on uncharted roads. Thus, when a number of observers (for example, Henry, 1949) have noted that successful businessmen often harbor a "fear of failure," they are not necessarily implying that such businessmen are abnormally neurotic (though, of course, some actually may be so).

The point is that all of us invoke mechanisms for reducing our feelings of uncertainty and tension. The ways in which we do attempt to lessen our anxieties are of critical importance and of great value in trying to understand why we behave the way we do.

THE MOTIVATIONAL DETERMINANTS OF ORGANIZATIONAL LEADERS

The questionnaire employed in this research has been designed primarily to measure the key personality variables of the basic typology (and a series of leadership and initiative-taking correlates that will be discussed in the following chapters). Yet it is equally important that an attempt be made to understand the underlying motivations that drive and direct the organizational behavior predicted by the typology. The questionnaire thus includes a thematic apperception test protocol (or TAT) specifically designed to tap subconscious motivations (or "motive dispositions") that help us understand the personal need systems of business and military leaders.[4] By making use of a growing body of research that has utilized the TAT instrument, the analysis of our leadership types is enriched by making reference to behavior not immediately testable with our subject populations.

The Motives to Be Utilized: The Power Motive

The power motive is associated with a distinctive personal history and certain traits of style that have been exhibited by a significant number, though not a majority, of elites in this study. People who have a high need for power tend to seek visibility through expressive modes of participation, have a capacity to form alliances when attempting to solve difficult problems, are competitive, will nurture interpersonal relationships for instrumental gain, act aggressively, are attracted to gambles that may yield large payoffs, and show unusual concern for maintaining influence over other people (McClelland and Steele, 1973; Winter, 1973). Chapter 4 will center around a discussion of the need for power and the way in which it affects most influentially the existential type of leader.

It is appropriate to distinguish between two forms of the power motive. First, observed by Freud, Adler, and Horney (Winter, 1973: 156-157) is positive or "social," power, which originates in the integrated ego; the second form of power is negative, or "personal," power, which stems from ego-related weaknesses. People who need personal power (or P power as it is sometimes called) try to dominate others from a fear of being dominated, while people driven by social power (or S power) show a strong concern for group goals and have great faith in people. Winter has concluded that a high need for personal power is associated with movements and professions that emphasize norms but do not require the changing of values.

Contrary to our expectations, it was the insecure leader who most often expressed a need for social power. Chapters 4 and 5 will explore the fundamental paradox that positive action can be taken for the betterment of the organization, though its motivational basis includes a component of basic insecurity.

The Need To Achieve

More than 20 years ago McClelland (1961) formulated the hypothesis that societies rise and fall as the psychological determination of their peoples to achieve grows and declines. Since that time literally hundreds of studies have been published using the "need for achievement" construct as measured through thematic apperception.

The need to achieve has been called a "psychological precondition" or motivation and has been shown to lead to a specific range of behavior. This behavior has been called entrepreneurial in nature and includes a propensity for innovative and energetic activity, a preference for systematic problem solving, a need for personal feedback, a desire for individual responsibility, moderate risk taking, and upward social mobility (Mc-Clelland, 1961; McClelland and Winter, 1969). Assessing the need to achieve among the leadership types will round out our understanding of the motivational basis of the four types and will allow us to predict modes of risk taking and the extent to which the types are predisposed toward innovative activity. It will also be of interest to examine whether bureaucracy provides adequate opportunity for the high need achiever to express himself.

The Need for Affiliation

In addition to the power motive and the need for achievement, our leaders express in varying degrees a need to be liked. A strong desire for "affiliation" is associated with conformity to the desires of others and the tendency to yield to social influence of all types. Individuals high in the need for affiliation exhibit an unusually strong fear of rejection, especially when in the public eye, yet are self-assertive, confident, and perceived by others as being egotistical. High levels of sociality and a need affiliative leadership style may provide the communicative skills requisite of one who is a successful "organization man"—the man who rises to the top of the pyramid. On the other hand, the fear of rejection that the need affiliative leader experiences and his high level of intense affective involvement often inhibit a detached style and the rational handling of power. Evidence to be presented in this work will illustrate how the need for affiliation can mitigate intiative taking in large organizations.

THE CONCEPT OF "WORLD VIEW": ITS IMPORTANCE IN EXPLAINING LEADERSHIP BEHAVIOR

The first task of this work has been to develop a leadership typology composed of the most powerful personality characteristics with which we are familiar and which we may measure with some degree of confidence. This effort has been described in the previous introductory sections and will be elaborated upon throughout this work. Our second task has been to predict a series of leadership style traits that cluster about each of the types. The critical step that unites the first and second tasks of the research process is the positing of distinct world views (and perceptual styles) for each of the types. It is the world view that brings together character and behavior.

Many traditions of social inquiry have investigated the relationship between world view and behavior. In the phenomenological tradition, Wittgenstein (1945) and Mannheim (1936) have noted how the impreciseness and nonuniversality of language contribute to misunderstanding and a general inability to comprehend the variety of cultures that surround us. Drawing from similar phenomenological sources of inspiration, Merleau-Ponty (Heider, 1958: 51) stated: "Our whole perception is pervaded by a logic which assigns to each object all its properties in relation to those of others, and which excludes as *unreal* any non-fitting information (italics added)." For these writers world view is inextricably bound up with, indeed dictated by, one's perceptual style, or the way in which one perceives the world.

Lippmann conjures up images of Plato's "Simile of the Cave" when he speaks of man's proclivity for processing incomplete, often incoherent and refracted bits of reality through the adaptive cognitive process of sterotypy. Lippmann (1965: 59-60) incisively states:

> In untrained observation we pick recognizable signs out of the environment. The signs stand for ideas and these ideas fill out with our stock of images ... the subtlest and most pervasive of all influences are those which create and maintain the repertory of stereotypes. We are told about the world before we see it. We imagine most things before we experience them. And these preconceptions ... govern deeply the whole process of perception. They mark out certain objects as familiar or strange, emphasizing the difference, so that the slightly familiar is seen as very familiar, and the somewhat strange as sharply alien. They are aroused by small signs, which may vary from a true index to a vague analogy. Aroused, they flood fresh vision with older images, and project into the world what has been resurrected in memory.

For Lippmann, man uses his opinions to mediate inner demands with outer experiences. By stereotyping or categorizing new information, we need not relive our original experience with that information nor do we need to understand it as something unique. The world outside creates "pictures in our heads." These pictures are for us our image of reality (however distorted) and our experience of the world.

In a different but not unrelated tradition, Harry Stack Sullivan has written extensively on the nature of perception and the many different socialization factors that color our view of the world. For Sullivan (Mullahay, 1968:297) each of us contains a dynamic or "instrumentality" by means of which experiences that are incongruous with our established mental framework become ignored, selectively unattended or dissociated. This instrumentality is called "antianxiety." The point is that Sullivan reserved a central place in his mature works for the notion that we all contain steering mechanisms that point us this way and that, diverting us from some incongruous thought, feeling, or overt action to a different one more congruent with the self. Our perceptive capabilities therefore define and delimit our understanding and our experience of the world.

In the present study world view may be defined broadly as our internalized picture of the world and the set of "givens" we take with us through life and invoke as mechanisms of understanding. As Robert Lane has written in *Political Ideology* (1967: 15), the notion of ideology (or world view, as we have here used the term) "entails a normative system of values, implies an empirical theory of cause and effect, and a theory of the nature of man."

A central goal of this study will be to characterize the world view of each leadership type by examining its unique conceptions of cause and effect and its beliefs about the nature of man. But, in order to conceptualize the world view that distinguishes each of the four types, we must identify the internal dynamics of each and demonstrate how these internal dynamics differ both quantitatively and qualitatively. Many of the following chapters will be devoted to this end.

PERSONALITY: AN INTERACTIVE HOLISTIC APPROACH

Our data strongly challenge the mass of simple bivariate monocausal studies that suggest that an experience of exogenous control produces ineffective, quiescent human beings. Our greatest activist and taker of initiatives, and perhaps our greatest leader, the existential man, is highly external. And, too, our greatest conformist (the administrator) is also our greatest need achiever. How are these seeming contradictions reconciled?

As we will show, a person is not just a "need achiever," a "power seeker," "externally located," "trusting," or any single quality. He is all these and much, much more that we do not know, in varying degrees. The existential leader experiences a feeling of being somehow controlled by outside forces, yet he is highly self-confident. Our administrative man experiences a strong need to achieve but he is also motivated by affiliation needs and plagued by personal insecurity. Human beings and the ways in which they think are often complex and seemingly contradictory. It is the interactive nature of the whole ensemble of personality relations that yields both explanatory and predictive power.

From the start we have viewed the task of this research as one of creatively reconstructing limited fragments of information. Conceptually, the task has been akin to placing together pieces of a complicated puzzle. The puzzle is complicated not so much because of the dizzying pattern of the known pieces, but because of the large (and unknown) number of missing pieces.

Simple monocausal explanations may be viewed as simple puzzles.

Let us use as an example simple locus of control research. While most researchers typically see the whole of personality as being either (and only) "internal" or "external" (as seen in Figure 2.2), "internality" or "externality" is in reality but a fragment of personality (see Figure 2.3). How can we predict a whole range of behaviors, such as leadership style, from looking at a fragment of personality?

The typical empirical view of personality is not holistic, but fragmented. It does not acknowledge the large number of unknown pieces or even tacitly admit that such pieces exist. Such a view as that taken in the above is responsible for perpetrating the myth that externality may be equated with an inability to function effectively in American society.[5]

McClelland's (1976) recent work, which focuses on the power motive and at the same time stresses "combinatorial motive systems," comes closer to a holistic view of human motivation as a determinant of behavior. McClelland sees the personality puzzle as consisting of need for achievement, need for affiliation, need for power, and inhibition. These are said to compose a motive dispositional system (see Figure 2.4). But the motive system itself is only part of the whole personality.

An even more holistic approach, the one advocated in this work, stresses multivariate interactions between motivations, self-image, and world view. It seeks to put more of the puzzle together by interconnecting more of the largest (and most meaningful) pieces (see Figure 2.5). The increase in available pieces and their logical placement in the schema of

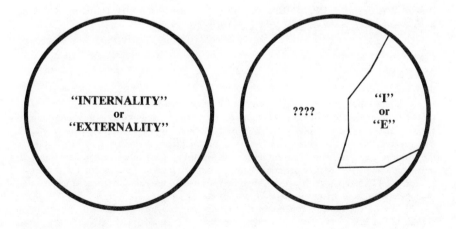

| Figure 2.2 | Figure 2.3 |
| Personality: Either This or That | Personality: A Fragment |

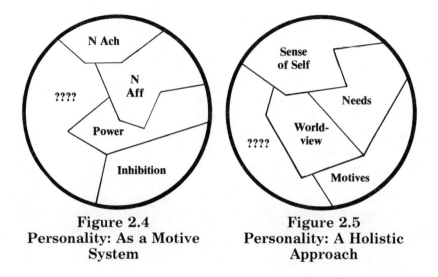

Figure 2.4
Personality: As a Motive
System

Figure 2.5
Personality: A Holistic
Approach

the whole picture yields a significantly greater and more holistic view of that picture, even though we are still missing an unknown number of pieces.

In attempting to predict ranges of behavior by looking at the puzzle, we must therfore account for our missing pieces and the place where each of our known pieces shall go.[6] By mapping the interrelations of a logical series of personality attributes we have attained greater explanatory power. Only when such a holistic approach is utilized can social scientists better understand the nature of man and the complex relationship that exists between personality and behavior.

NOTES

1. If the typology developed in this work were used to describe general personality types found outside, as well as inside, organizations, it might well be that in this first quadrant we would find not only rational men but "passive-certain" men as well. The passive-certain is not common to American society but has been spawned far more in Eastern cultures, often in the form of the guru—the self-confident, contemplative, constantly working for inner self-improvement person who is generally content and unconcerned with events in the world around him. Our typology, however, shall be confined to the categorization of leaders and managers who are denizens of large organizations.

2. Among the military officers in this group are six who have been promoted in an accelerated fashion.

3. Weber as sociologist devoted much attention to the institutional mechanisms that promoted leadership. Thus, he was interested in the concept of "legitimacy" and its legal, charismatic, and historical forms. Only in the *Protestant Ethic and the Spirit of Captialism* does Weber centrally concern himself with the psychology of leadership.

4. The three pictures used in the questionnaire will be presented in Chapters 4 and 6. A discussion of the methods of administering and scoring the pictures appears in Appendix III.

5. Other disciplines have long stressed the need for viewing persons and their relations by a holistic approach. Erikson (1973), for example, sees no other way to understand human development. And, similarly, Raymond Aron (1960) has called it "imperative" to study historical developments as "whole ensembles of relations." At the microlevel (as in the study of personality) the need for using the holistic approach is equally compelling.

6. Statisticians merely say, "Let's account for more of the variance."

CHAPTER 3

RATIONAL MAN

The bureaucratic leader who is self-confident and experiences a near-total sense of control is both active and certain. His near-total sense of certainty as it is projected toward his environment, and as introjected toward the sense of self, actuates a particularly "rational" style of leadership. This chapter will examine the character, world view, and behavior of our first leader, the rational man.

Rational man lives in a world made up of logical, predictable, and orderly relations. The daily problems with which he is faced have solutions—his primary task is to find them. Rational man lives in a rational world. In contrast to other kinds of power-oriented leaders (such as our existential man), our rational man does not often use strong-arm or interpersonal influence tactics. His leadership style reflects a friendly but strongly goal-directed orientation. His amiable relations with others are an outgrowth of his understanding of the world: "People do things for reasons—understand people's motivations, and you will understand people. The world isn't threatening. Trust your fellow workers and be trusted. Together, we can both attain success."

The rational man strives for success, and does so intensely. Yet, unlike other kinds of leaders, he does not allow his stab at success to run rampant over other personal concerns. The rational man believes that solving problems rather than controlling people is the surest strategy for the attainment of success. A world of order need only be understood to be conquered.

THE RATIONAL MAN AND HIS SENSE OF SELF

The rational man thrives in an intrapsychic world of relative comfort. He experiences no dissonance concerning his ability to achieve, for there is a strong coincidence between his aspirations and his achievements. Being very high in self-esteem, he reacts to new situations with expectations of success, since characteristically he has been successful in the past with achieving his goals. It is this "expectancy of succeeding" that is the guiding principle of the rational man.

The rational man experiences a very strong sense of personal control—that is, control both over his own impulses and his work environment. Since he believes he can, and does, exercise control over his world, he believes his actions will make a difference. He therefore enjoys his work and believes it has meaning. Confidence in the ability to achieve continued success, coupled with confidence in the capacity to control, allows this type of leader to act with certainty. His actions are thus purposive, his goals far-reaching.

Table 3.1 illustrates the elevated sense of self and the strong feeling of control that characterize, indeed define, rational man. As is apparent from the table, the rational man experiences significantly more self-confidence and control than either the business or military elite as a whole. (And we must here remind the reader that these elites are successful professionals marked by an abundance of these two qualities.)

Let us now find out how these two qualities are likely to affect the behavior of our rational man.

Table 3.1: Rational Man: His Level of Self-Esteem and Locus of Control*

Group	Self-Esteem				Locus of Control			
	N	$\bar{X}$	t	$p\ value$	N	$\bar{X}$	t	$p\ value$
Rational Man	43	84.99			43	4.09		
		(SD= 3.10)				(SD=1.52)		
Whole Business	62	70.17	9.32	.001	58	9.01	−9.56	.001
Elite		(SD=10.02)				(SD=3.10)		
Whole Military	223	71.56	9.12	.001	198	8.98	−8.42	.001
Elite		(SD= 9.48)				(SD=3.73)		

*All t tests of means reported in this book are two-tailed unless otherwise indicated. Respondents who did not complete all items in each scale were omitted from the analyses. Missing or incomplete responses do not appear in this or any subsequent tables.

HIGH SELF-ESTEEM AND THE EXPERIENCE OF CONTROL: RESEARCH FINDINGS

Several studies conducted by Hovland and Janis (1959) have revealed that people who experience strong feelings of self-esteem are better able to resist the pressures of social influence, and especially the pressure to conform. Other studies have also shown that persons of high self-esteem tend to be more assertive and domineering and at the same time have a desire for prestige and personal independence.

While literally hundreds of researchers have studied the effects of an internal perception of control, and it is assumed that internals are the real achievers in American society, very few findings have been unequivocally replicated.[1] In general, it may be said that internals have been found to be goal-directed, high in self-esteem, domineering, sociable, and capable of resisting influence attempts by others. Summary Tables 3.2 and 3.3 illustrate some important personality correlates of high self-esteem and belief in the ability to control one's fate as reported by other researchers.

What do our own data tell us about the rational man and his twofold sense of control and self confidence? Our findings indicate strong congruence with the literature: When compared with either the whole business or military population, the rational man is at the same time dominant, active, persuasive, extroverted, and, as we shall see, goal-directed.[2]

Responses to survey questions that distinguish between rational man's perceived ability to control his own personal actions and the actions of others in his environment also reveal that this leader believes he has the ability to control other people. Not a single rational leader perceives systemic forces as significantly affecting his movement through the organization. Opportunity for such movement, he believes, is based soley on personal motivations and capabilities to the exclusion of chance, luck, fate, or other indeterminate and fatalistic unknowns.[3]

The consequences of this orientation are twofold: First, rational man is not influenced, or otherwise significantly affected, by the possibility of unknown forces acting against his desired outcomes. The belief that personal causation is paramount, together with a very strong sense of self-confidence, allows this leader to assume an unwavering and unremitting posture of certainty. His reasoning behind this posture is rational: "For me success is determined by the extent of my desires and capabilities. I have been successful at all I have done in the past, and if I try hard enough, I will continue to achieve success in the future."

The second consequence of this high self-esteem-internal orientation is that the rational man does not experience an anxiety-ridden or threatening world. His world makes sense. It is constant and logical. And

Table 3.2: Correlates of High Self-Esteem

Characteristic	Source
Does not strive for positions of power	Lasswell (1930, 1948)
Greater leadership potential, self acceptance	Bills, et al. (1951)
Has a strong need for high status	Gough (1956) (cited in MacDonald, 1973)
Exhibits the ability to persuade others, resists influence attempts by others	Hovland and Janis (1959)
Often rejects new information, shows symptoms of being closed-minded	Byrne (1961)
Exhibits psychological "health"	Fitts (Reported in Crandall, 1973)
Displays assertiveness, stability	Rosenberg (1965)
Displays strong political involvement; activity orientation	Barber (1965); Milbrath and Klein (1962)
Has higher sociometric status (is viewed more positively by others)	Ziller, et al. (1969)
Displays dominance	Hamilton (1971)
Shows open-mindedness	Hamilton (1971); Rokeach (1960)
Exhibits less anxiety and less neurotic behavior (than persons of low self-esteem); performs more effectively under stress	Wells and Marwell (1976)

since a rational world is penetrable by understanding, it is not threatening or conspiratorial. It merely presents manifold problems that await solution. These problems have no valence. Fates, if they do exist, are not malevolent, but susceptible to control.

MOTIVATIONAL DETERMINANTS

As measured through use of the three-picture TAT protocol, rational man displayed only a moderate need for power.[4] This type of leader relies not so much on interpersonal power tactics (such as controlling or distorting information or coercing subordinates by use of threats), as he prefers a complex pattern of both trust and compliance-expectation based on his own personal history of goal accomplishment. The rational man works with and trusts others when trying to get ahead and anticipates and

Table 3.3: Correlates of an Internal Locus of Control

Characteristic	Source
Do better under conditions of skill, while "externals" do well under conditions of chance	Lefcourt (1965)
Perceive strong control over their destiny	Rotter (1966)
Capacity for resisting influence attempts by others	Rotter (1966)
Show more independence of judgement	Lefcourt (1966)
Show less anxiety	Watson (1967); Hountras and Scharf (1970)
Are academically successful; score higher on achievement tests	McGhee and Crandall (1968); Lao (1970); Messer (1972)
Come from "warm, democratic homes where nurturance is combined with principled discipline, predictable standards"	Davis and Phares (1969); MacDonald (1971)
Goal-directedness, "instrumentality"	MacDonald (1973)
Strong self-esteem	Fish and Karabenick (1971); Ryckman and Sherman (1972)
Dominance	Hersch and Scheibe (1967)
Display more cautious risk-taking behavior	Joe (1971)

expects that others will carry out his directives—recourse to power tactics is not "needed."

The rational man neither mistrusts others nor fears for the loss of his formal organizational base of power (two potentially great motivating forces). Self-report measures indicate that rational man trusts superiors and subordinates alike, while projective measures provide some convergent evidence and indicate that the rational man displays very little subconscious fear of other powerful people in the organization.[5] Interestingly enough, however, the rational man does not subconsciously express a strong "hope" of gaining more power than he already has. In fact, less than any of the three other leadership types does the rational man desire power for the satisfaction of his most salient personality needs. Rational man seeks not to control people but to solve problems. Comfortable with his high status and secure in the knowledge that he will attain even more, the rational man is a leader who is interested in gaining power, though it is apparent that he displays no preoccupation with that end.

That rational man is not fascinated with or consumed by the pursuit of power is evident from Table 3.4. As well as comparing rational man's need for power (as measured through unconscious motivation) with that of the whole business and military elite, the table also presents scored TAT stories written by two groups of people who did not participate in this study. These groups consist of 50 business managers and 60 college students. The business managers are employed by a large, well-known corporation, while the college student sample consists of people currently attending a prestigious liberal arts institution. Both the managers and the students wrote stories in response to the identical three TAT pictures used in the present study, and scoring of the stories was done by the same independent contractor using the identical methodological procedures.[6] Comparative evidence indicates that indeed, when compared with either his elite colleagues or other people in the population at large, rational man displays moderate power needs. His desire to impress others is not ascendant over other more strongly held predispositions.

Along with his moderate need for power, the rational man also has a moderate (and healthy) need to "affiliate," or work with others. What is distinctive about this type of leader is that all his personal qualities show up in moderation. He is, by nature, a moderate, even-tempered man whose affiliative concerns do not interfere with his goal-directedness. For example, when solving occupational problems, he chooses the help of experts and not friends (this maximizes his chances for success). Yet the rational man does not eschew friends and loved ones when off the job.

Table 3.4: Need for Power Among Rational Men and Samples of Business Managers and College Students*

Group	N	Need Power $\bar{X}$	Need Power SD	Fear of Power $\bar{X}$	Fear of Power SD	Hope for Power $\bar{X}$	Hope for Power SD
Rational Men	37	2.78	3.95	0.51	1.21	1.16	2.04
Whole Business Elite	51	3.54	3.93	0.37	1.18	1.47	1.60
Whole Military Elite	175	2.86	3.33	0.62	1.35	1.26	1.74
Business Managers	50	4.78	NA	NA	NA	NA	NA
College Students	60	6.38	NA	NA	NA	NA	NA

*Mean differences between rational men and the whole business and military elite groups are not statistically significant at the .05 level. In order for TATs to be counted as valid, respondents had to write stories consisting of at least one paragraph. Respondents who did not do so were omitted from this and all subsequent analyses employing the TAT. The reader is referred to Appendix III for a brief discussion of the relationship between word length of stories written and scored incidences of achievement, power, and affiliation. Because of differing test conditions, interstudy comparisons should be interpreted with caution.

NA indicates data were unavailable.

Evidence presented in Chapter 4 indicates that he suffers no "afflictions of the heart" as does Maccoby's (1976) "gamesman."

What is equally distinctive about the motivations of rational man is his strong need to achieve. Coupled with his strong experience of personal control, the rational man feels and exudes great confidence in his ability to affect or change his work environment.[7] These feelings of confidence are picked up by superiors and subordinates alike and contribute to his image as a leader who can be trusted.

The belief that the outcomes of his actions are directly related to the content of those actions and not to the influence of some intervening exogenous force apparently strengthens feelings of efficacy and encourages goal-directed achieving behavior. At the same time, the rational man's need for achievement mitigates his power strivings. When one is certain that his actions will produce his desired outcomes, he need not use force for the attainment of that end.[8]

THE RATIONAL MAN AND SUPERIOR-SUBORDINATE RELATIONS

Upon entering a profession many people have an idea of what it is they would like to become. Other people do not and just make the most of opportunities that come their way. When the rational man was asked, "Upon entrance to your profession, did you have a clear picture of what position or rank you wanted to attain?" more than 30 percent said they had "a very clear picture." Another 55 percent said they had a picture, though it was "unclear." As a group, the rational man shows the greatest number of leaders who reported such clarity of vision. This ability to envision clearly what he wants to become may suggest that the rational man is occupationally aggressive. When he is asked if he has (at present) attained his desired position, less than one in four says he has. This becomes particularly meaningful when we note that among this group of leaders we find seven directors of large corporations and twelve full colonels. While the rational man maintains an expectancy of future success, he does not sit idly by in the hope of somehow attaining it without purposive action. He vigorously pursues success through goal-directed, rational activity.

The drive toward the attainment of high status manifests itself in the everyday work of the rational man. As we would predict from his unwavering posture of self-confidence, the rational man scores considerably higher than his elite colleagues on our measure of "activity-passivity".[9] And, consistent with his active and achievement-oriented nature, the rational man presents superiors with unsolicited recommendations more often than any other leadership type (save the existential man) and most often feels that these recommendations will be acted upon (another manifestation of his strong self-confidence and his expectancy of success). See Tables 3.5 and 3.6.

When describing the motivations of rational man, we said he had a very moderate need for personal power and a healthy balance of the need to affiliate with others. Table 3.7 illustrates that this even temperament is reflected in his trusting relations with superiors and subordinates.

An interesting view of the nature of trust has been developed by Riker, who believes that trust involves risk, since the people in whom one has decided to depend may or may not prove worthy. "Prior to the trusting decision," states Riker (1974) "we have necessarily . . . assessed the risk of trusting and have decided that the risk is worth taking." The rational man experiences an interpersonal environment of comparatively low risk in that (1) he has the utmost confidence in his ability to elicit compliant behavior from his subordinates (an "expectancy of success"), and (2) like all formal organizational powerholders, the rational man holds official powers of authority that accrue to him by virtue of his position in the chain of command and that he may utilize in the form of official sanctions and rewards. For rational man, both private perceptions and role-derived sanctions act in concert to mitigate the need for both risk taking and the domination of others.

While the rational man is both dominant and persuasive (two qualities measured by use of semantic differentials), his leadership style is by no means authoritarian or unusually inflexible. More than any other leadership type, the rational man agreed with the statement "a good leader expects his subordinates to decide for themselves what they should be doing." Unlike other kinds of leaders who believe that subordinates should be told precisely what to do, the rational man does not seek to control others, but works with them in order to increase his own chances for success.

While the rational man is concerned with solving work-related problems, his strategy for the attainment of personal goals does not normally involve the manipulation or use of others. For example, the rational man is not so enveloped in his work that he can't spend some time engaging in political conversation. More than any of the other leadership types, the rational man exhibits "opinion leadership" qualities having tried most often to convince others of his political convictions.[10] The outgoing and confident nature of our rational man creates an image that is likeable to both superiors and subordinates. His altruistic world, his "rationality" (and not his emotionality), and his trusting nature encourage people to see this leader as one who is always willing to give sound advice. Not surprisingly, therefore, our evidence reveals that the rational man is queried often about the nature of his personal political convictions.

Table 3.5: "How often do you present superiors with unsolicited recommendations?" (%)

Group	N	Always	Very Often	Often	Not Very Often
Rational Man	43	4.7	60.5	32.6	2.3
Whole Business Elite	63	7.9	54.0	36.5	1.6
Whole Military Elite	226	3.5	45.6	38.9	11.9

$X^2 = 14.03$, p $< .08$.

Table 3.6: "When you do present superiors with unsolicited recommendations, usually how certain are you that these recommendations will be acted upon?" (%)

Group	N	Very Certain	Certain	Somewhat Certain	Not Very Certain
Rational Man	43	18.6	58.1	18.6	4.7
Whole Business Elite	63	7.9	47.6	33.3	11.1
Whole Military Elite	226	7.1	34.5	37.6	20.7

$X^2 = 25.48$, p. $< .01$.

37

Table 3.7: Rational Man: His Sense of Trust*

Group	Interpersonal Trust				Trust in Subordinates			Trust in Superiors		
	N	$\bar{X}$	t	p value	$\bar{X}$	t	p value	X	t	p value
Rational Man	42	67.60 (SD = 10.14)			69.02 (SD = 9.09)			65.58 (SD = 15.51)		
Whole Business Elite	59	64.44 (SD = 11.41)	1.46	.14	66.96 (SD = 10.31)	1.06	NS	62.29 (SD = 15.90)	1.05	NS
Whole Military Elite	224	62.47 (SD = 9.29)	3.04	.004	64.46 (SD = 9.84)	2.94	.005	69.93 (SD = 11.81)	2.72	.007

*Data presented in this table are summed (and normalized) scores on an eight-question trust scale. Trust in superiors and trust in subordinates are presented as separable dimensions. Seven respondents failed to complete all eight items of the scale. They were omitted from this and subsequent analyses.

38

The Need for Encouragement

The rational man views his superiors and subordinates not only as trustworthy but as trusting. Rather than displaying behavior aimed at satisfying personal interests, the rational man believes his superiors and subordinates are generally responsive to organizational needs and goals. Paradoxically, the rational man needs and receives little encouragement from the associates in whom he places his trust and prefers to be encouraged (however infrequently) by his friends made outside the organization. This aspect of his need system is consistent with the theory of the self-starter.

While the rational man needs little encouragement from others, he does feel strongly that his accomplishments must be recognized by others. This rather strong desire for recognition is another piece of evidence that while it does not detract from his "activity-certainty," does limit his capacity as a driven self-starter. For the true self-starter is one who is continuously, almost automatically self-motivated. The differing kinds of affective cues he receives from others (either before, during, or after the initiative-taking endeavor) do not affect the nature of his behavior or deter his impulse to act.

While the rational man is not interpersonally cold or aloof, his style is one that minimizes affectual and power-oriented entanglements. His primary motivation is the attainment of organizational goals and not the attainment of purely personal power.[11] But this leader is not a conformist; this leader is an "organizational loyalist," whose duty to his organization supersedes affective ties to individuals. Said one rational man (a major who attended the Air War College): "At work, the important thing is the job, not who does it." Goal-directedness and an abiding faith in the organization that has served him so well thus displaces the emotional involvement displayed by Lasswell's (1930) "administrator" or other kinds of leaders such as Barber's (1972) "active-negative." To a very large extent it can be seen that the rational man resembles Anthony Downs' (1967) conception of the "utility maximizer." He very much fits the rational man model of bureaucratic leadership, his utilitarianism as a guide to action. As such, however, he falls prey to the irrational pitfalls of rational men. (We shall explore this theme more fully at the close of this chapter.)

THE RATIONAL MAN AS SELF-STARTER

In Chapters 1 and 2 the notion of the self-starter was briefly developed. It was hypothesized that the self-starter was driven by anxiety, either about achieving or controlling. Ambiguity or anxiety, we reasoned, would serve as a drive factor or a catalyst for action. The rational man, it was hypothesized, could not be a true self-starter—for his general sense of comfort, we speculated, would distill any compulsion to innovate or take initiative unless such behavior was judged to result in "success."

Throughout this work we will be interested in exploring Lasswell's hypothesis that (organizational) initiative taking is the result of active attempts at eradicating feelings of insecurity. In the case of the rational man, we seem to be confronted with Lasswell's "null hypothesis." Here we may ask, can initiative taking and attempts at bureaucratic innovation be associated with (or derive from) feelings of self-esteem and a general state of psychological "health"? Does psychological well-being "free" the leader from potentially debilitating anxieties and allow him to act with certainty for the betterment of his organization? Let us examine this null hypothesis more closely.

RATIONAL MAN IS PSYCHOLOGICALLY UNBURDENED: HE FEELS FREE TO ACT

Almost 55 percent of our rational men said they enjoyed competition "very much." This was well above the combined norm for the whole population of business and military elites, professionals who are competitive by nature. As indicated, the rational man is a great seeker of challenges. Available evidence presented thus far shows that challenge seeking (one very important self-starter behavior) need not be the manifestation of personal insecurity or anxiety. As much of the published literature in the areas of self-esteem and locus of control theory would predict, positive self-regard and a strong perception of control apparently encourage frequent attempts at acting on the environment.[12] Challenge seeking is but one expression of this active orientation toward the world.

The availability of challenges to be sought can differ from organization to organization and with regard to current assignment or position held within the organization. Such structural irregularities can certainly affect responses to the question posed in Table 3.8. However, we see that there is a significant difference between the propensity of the rational man to seek challenges and the frequency of challenge seeking among his elite colleagues.

Despite possible disparities then with respect to the availability of challenges to be sought, it is clear that the rational man spends a good deal of his time seeking out challenges. His perception is that these challenges are worth seeking, that challenges can have useful results, and that these results will be recognized by the organization. The rational man pursues action because he feels particularly efficacious—he believes he has the power to produce effects.

Table 3.8: "How often do you actively seek out new challenges?" (%)

Group	N	Always	Very Often	Often	Not Very Often	Infrequent
Rational Man	43	25.6	46.5	23.3	2.3	2.3
Whole Business Elite	63	14.8	27.5	15.7	4.5	0.0
Whole Military Elite	226	5.3	35.4	40.7	18.1	0.4

$X^2 = 50.03$, p. $< .001$.

Frequent challenge seeking is a salient aspect of both rational man's leadership style and his strategy for getting ahead. Yet there is a great difference between seeking out challenges in the environment and creating one's own challenges. For example, it is common lore among professional athletes that one of the greatest differences between players who make it and those who do not is that the successful athlete creates his own opportunities. Great ball players not only exploit opportunities that come their way but they make breaks come their way. Similarly, the organizational leader may respond primarily to challenges that come across his desk, or he may, if ambitious enough, seek to create challenges never even conceived by others.

Does the rational man create challenges for himself, or does he respond primarily to challenges offered him by his environment? Our evidence indicates that most of our elites actively seek to create challenges. This, of course, is a key to their organizational success. While there are differences between the two parent populations (as well as differentials in opportunity and reward structures), Table 3.9 shows that the greater initiative displayed by the rational man is in evidence.[13]

In psychological terms, the style that the rational man uses in his pursuit of success is the result of his acting on private and type-specific needs—his very experience and view of the world enable him to pursue power by utilizing rational, goal-directed strategies.

The rational man achieves and controls. He feels his actions will make a difference. His purposiveness is not distorted by a world view of encroaching subordinates, jealous superiors, fear of failure, or fear of success. The problems that he encounters have solutions. Both superiors and subordinates can be trusted to work with him in finding those solutions. The ease with which the rational man relates to others and the respect they apparently show him[14] allows us to infer that this leader is capable of effective alliance building and group goal facilitation (McClelland and Steele, 1973).

Our theory of the continuously motivated leader postulates that as a self-starter he needs little encouragement in the course of his work. The impulse to do (while subject to differing ecological reward structures) is continuously manifest despite the organization to which the self-starter belongs and whether at work or at leisure. How well does the rational man conform to our ideal image of the continuously motivated self-starter?

Perhaps an examination of why the rational man seeks and enjoys new challenges may provide us with an answer. Maccoby (1976) and McClelland and Burnham (1976) have noted that different kinds of managers adopt problem-solving modes that are congruent with their general perception of reality. For example, McClelland has found that

Table 3.9: "Would you consider yourself a person who actively looks for challenges or someone who becomes motivated primarily through challenges that appear on your desk?" (%)

Group	N	"I actively look for challenges"	"I become motivated by challenges that appear on my desk"
Rational Man	43	86.0	9.3
Whole Business Elite	63	77.8	20.6
Whole Military Elite	226	69.9	28.3

$X^2 = 7.36$, p. $< .03$.

people high in the need for power attempt solutions to challenges (or problems) that can create impact or provide a strong impression on others. Their risk-taking behavior as well is oriented toward creating impact or securing the big payoff. Similarly, when given a choice to win money by either gambling or solving paper-and-pencil problems, people with a strong need for achievement would prefer to solve problems. What McClelland has tried to show is that individuals select a problem-solving mode that is consistent with their most basic personality needs (or dispositions).

The rational man seeks out challenges because the successful accomplishment of the challenge gives him great pleasure. Unlike some need achievers and some technicians, the rational man does not particularly enjoy the problem-solving process. He does not derive any special satisfaction from merely making inroads in pursuit of a difficult solution. He cares little for incremental gain. The rational man is gratified purely by the culmination of the act. The solution itself, and not the search for the solution, is the essence of his professional satisfaction.

The rational man does not enjoy working on challenging problems for any intrinsic reason. At the same time, and consistent with his personality needs, he doesn't especially enjoy the prestige of being confronted with tough challenges that others would shy away from (the existential man, on the other hand, does). In order of importance, then, the rational man enjoys new problems (1) because the successful accomplishment of the problem gives him great pleasure; (2) the process of problem solving (for its own sake) is personally rewarding; and (3) the prestige that accrues to one who responds to tough challenges or problems is satisfying.[15]

Unlike other types of self-starters, then, the rational man feels no need to do or continuously self-actuate. While he does act on his environment, his actions are determined not so much by motivations that can be conceived of as process-oriented, as by a meaningful sense of personal accomplishment that he enjoys upon completion of the goal-directed task.

The rational man does not take initiative because of some inner compulsion to reshape his environment or reconcile some private inadequacies. The rational man is much the utilitarian. The successful completion of the challenge is an end in itself. Initiative taking is a strategy by which his present position or status may be maintained and his future enhanced. (For the other three leadership types, initiative-taking is a means to reduce or otherwise distill personal anxieties and insecurities.) The seeking of challenges is thus not for the rational man a compensatory behavior deriving from some perceived inadequacy; it is a premeditated, instrumental, and rational strategy to get ahead—it is not an "impulse" to do.

WHEN THE RATIONAL MAN IS FACED
WITH SITUATIONAL AMBIGUITY

While the rational man does often present superiors with unsolicited recommendations and suggestions and while he is extremely confident that these recommendations will be acted upon, curiously enough, this leader does not feel particularly comfortable about making decisions that lack clear organizational ground rules or precedents (see Table 3.10). This feeling of discomfort is consistent with our portrayal of this leader as a rational man. That is, he is one who functions most effectively in an environment that provides him with factual information, the stuff of rational calculation. When information is imperfect or completely non-existent, the rational man is far less comfortable. Table 3.11 demonstrates that, his high self-esteem notwithstanding, this leader is unable to act comfortably under conditions of disorder. His limited ability to make decisions that lack organizational precedent results from his overall feelings of control and his essentially uninhibited, active nature.

Rather than making a bold, perhaps risky decision, the rational man goes with his proven formula of success and its well-tried operational code.[16] Rather than making an irrational mistake, he defers judgment to others and does not try to create the new precedent. Rational man's inability (or lack of desire) to make the most of situations that lack clearly defined normative courses of action lends a conservative bent to his overall leadership style.

Though he is somewhat conservative, rational man does not often engage in professional activity purely out of a sense of duty. All respondents were asked to answer the following question: "Americans today

Table 3.10: "How comfortable do you feel in making decisions about which there exist no organizational ground rules?" (%)

Group	N	Very Uncomfortable	Uncomfortable	Slightly Uncomfortable	Not at all Uncomfortable
Rational Man	43	18.6	0.0	25.6	53.5
Whole Business Elite	63	7.9	6.3	41.3	44.4
Whole Military Elite	224	4.0	4.0	52.2	38.8

$\chi^2 = 23.80$, p. $< .002$.

Table 3.11: Rational Man: The Relationship Between His Personality and the Ability to Make Decisions that Lack Organizational Ground Rules (N = 43)

Personality Characteristic	Beta Coefficient
Self-esteem	−.43*
Internal locus of control	.33*
Moderate need for achievement	−.01
Moderate need for affiliation	.26
Moderate need for power	.31*
Low inhibition	.40*
High activity	.15
Moderate trust	.29*

$R^2 = .23*$
$F = 2.29$

*$p < .05$

R squares in this and subsequent tables are adjusted.

are preoccupied with finding meaning in their lives and in their jobs. How often do you find your work personally meaningful, and how often just a duty?" The rational men as a group contained the greatest number of leaders who felt their work was personally meaningful and the smallest number who saw their work as a duty.[17]

His overall feelings of comfort, both with himself as a person and as a leader, do not cause the rational man to be quietistic. At the same time the motivations that drive his initiative-taking behavior do not have their foundation in a sense of anxiety or insecurity. Because the rational man fears neither success, failure, nor powerful others, he is psychologically free to act on his creative or instrumental desires.

The evidence presented in this chapter is not wholly supportive of our initial self-starter hypothesis—that self-starters are leaders who are driven by some form of anxiety. As we have seen, the rational man is much the self-starter—he selects his own goals, he enjoys competition, he seeks challenges very frequently, and he actively creates challenges. As well, he presents superiors with unsolicited recommendations and as inferred from his motive system, he displays goal-directed, achievement-oriented behavior. But, above all, the rational man is an initiative-taker (only) when it will result in some instrumental (material) gain.

Anxiety, then (among some kinds of leaders), appears not to be the necessary psychological precondition for the taking of initiatives. Initiative-taking activity for the rational man is not compensatory. Rather it is more the result of a healthy desire to achieve more success through oft-proven and organizationally (as well as socially) approved and valued strategies.

THE RATIONAL MAN: IS HE A LEADER OR A MANAGER?

While we are not yet able to determine if leaders and managers differ with respect to personality, it is apparent that the rational man is a "leader." Let us briefly speculate as to some possible differences between leaders and managers.

The extroverted, confident, and apparently likable manner that characterizes the rational man, his opinion leadership qualities and his ability to facilitate organizational goals without having to use others, indicates he is very much a leader (his formal status, of course, indicates he is a "manager" of some kind). The rational man feels very comfortable directing others and, as we have shown, feels more strongly than all other leadership types that his subordinates respect him in his decision-making role.

Perhaps leaders are uninhibited men of expansive egos who are able to act out, or live out, their personal needs. Managers, by contrast, may be people whose sense of self-control make them especially adept at operationalizing extant policy by reinforcing existing norms. Managerial self-control, we may hypothesize, inhibits innovative or risk-taking behavior requisite of the dynamic leader.

We have by no means fully developed the distinction between leaders and managers. Drawing more explicit differences between the two will be a task of later chapters.

THE PARADOX OF RATIONAL MAN:
RATIONAL MAN AS REALITY TESTER

Like all people the rational man "selects" signals in his environment that are consistent with strongly held beliefs both about himself and his vision of the world. Yet the ubiquitous sense of certainty and control experienced by rational man contains an illogical and irrational element. Other studies of powerful executives have noted an element of irrationality that has its basis in very high self-esteem and the experience of near total control. For example, Bartolomé (1972: 64) has noted that among business executives "the desire to avoid or ignore experience which the (executive) unconsciously perceives as damaging to his concept of himself appears to be quite strong." In the group that Bartolomé studied (as in our group of rational men), a strong sense of certainty was found to produce a potentially blinding "coping mechanism"—that of ignoring either the element of chance or information that conflicts with the rational sense of self.

Another series of studies deriving from a different tradition has shown that persons high in self-esteem most often employ avoidance defense mechanisms in the face of unpredictable or unanticipated outcomes (Byrne, 1961; Hovland and Janis, 1959). Such persons respond to failure in ways that either avoid self-evaluation or actually enhance their self-image. Through the use of these mechanisms, persons high in self-esteem are able to maintain their self-confidence and their psychological equilibrium.

People with a very strong sense of positive self-regard have, therefore, been shown to reject the assimilation of knowlege that can actually improve performance. This mode of rejection is the price of sound "health", for an enhanced or maintained view of the self as efficacious even in the face of occasional failure contributes to one's stability.

We have little reason to believe that the rational man's boundless certainty is based on a lifelong success rate significantly different from that of the other elite professionals whom we have studied. His notion of certainty is based on a purely subjective perception of success and the effective distortion of any incoming information that may contradict this perception. As an exceptionally elevated sense of self-esteem can blind a person from recognizing his human frailties, so too can a very strongly held belief in the ability to control one's fate or an overreliance on the application of logic and rationality.

In his recent book Edgar Schein (1978) also illustrates how self-esteem and rationality can combine to make life difficult for the ambitious organizational leader. He cites two examples of highly educated aerospace and manufacturing managers who fancied themselves rational men. Said the aerospace manager: "I thought I could sell people with logic and was amazed at the hidden agendas people have, *irrational* objections; really bright people will come up with stupid excuses . . . they have their own little empires to worry about" (p. 95, italics added). Said the manufacturing executive: "Quantification and an analytic approach is threatening to the senior man because it displaces his sense of experience" (p. 105). The wonderment expressed by these managers is naive. Of course people have hidden agendas and irrational objections; of course people are building empires. Logic and analysis are only part of the game.[18]

Similarly, the element of chance has long been recognized as key to the success of man. Machiavelli, following the ancients, reserved a central place in both the *Discourses* and *The Prince* for the concept of "fortuna." And Mosca (1939: 433), author of *The Ruling Class*, probably the most complete treatment of elites ever written, was forced to conclude that the role of chance was critical to the rise of elites:

> Many contingent factors show their influence in the choice of a particular individual for a high position, *and they operate at given moments only.* Such would be the prevalence of this or that political doctrine, or the way the few who already occupy high positions happen to feel about this or that person. *Always in the offing* is the element that may be called 'chance', which is merely another name for the unforeseeable (italics added).

Or, continues Mosca (1939: 457), " . . . the game of life, after all, is not so different from an ordinary game of cards, where winning depends now on blind chance, now on the skill of the player, now on the mistakes of the adversary."

In our own study we may cite the example of the president of an international electronics firm. He would be foolish to believe that only his expertise or continued attention could prevent marketplace or even political forces from acting on his product (computers). Similarly, in a clearly delineated chain of command such as is found in the military, a ranking officer may continually be subject to tour changes despite personal desires, likes, or dislikes.

One officer in this study (who is not a rational man) attributed "a few lucky breaks" to his achievement of high occupational success. Locus of control theorists might think this attribution indicates a sense of externality. Yet this officer went on to explain that if it were not for his assignment to a particular post, he never would have had the opportunity to finish his advanced degree, and perhaps he never would have been selected for command school (his entree into the highest echelon of his organization). Another officer, when asked if good leaders are born and not made, replied, "Maybe good leaders are born, but good managers are made." This officer is also able to recognize that luck (or fate) and personal capabilities bear on one's attainment of success.[19] And finally, Julian Rotter (1966: 4) has said:

> While it seems likely that the individuals at both extremes of the internal versus external control of reinforcement dimension are essentially *unrealistic,* it is not as likely that the people toward the middle are less confident. We do have indications, however, that the people at either extreme of the (fate-control) dimension are likely to be maladjusted by most definitions, and, to the extent that ego control is another type of definition of maladjustment, it would bear some curvilinear relationship to the variable we are concerned with here (locus of control) (italics added).

It is surely possible that circumstances beyond our control or our immediate field of vision can affect our greatest achievements. Inability to recognize this can limit our scope of vision and distort a realistic under-standing of the world around us. In short, it is not clear that powerholders who experience strong control of their environments are indeed in tune with the nature of the real world. While some leaders are better able than others to impose control where there exists disorder, it is clear that the elements of chance and timeliness are of significant import. The rational man runs the risk of blinding himself to that slice of reality (however thick or thin) that is subject to manipulation by forces unknown to him—forces that may affect his field of vision both as a person and as an organizational leader.

OVERVIEW OF THE RATIONAL MAN

Our first type of organizational leader feels exceptionally self-confident and in control of both his own actions and emotions. Not only is his sense of control directed toward himself but this type of leader feels he can control his work environment (including other people in the organi-zation). Table 3.12 shows that rational man is a high need achiever who experiences little personal anxiety and a strong sense of interpersonal trust.

These personality attributes encourage the active seeking of chal-

Table 3.12: Rational Man: His Character and Behavior

Character	Behavior
High in self-esteem	Actively seeks challenges
Belief in personal causation	Actively creates challenges
Dominant	Goal-directedness
Extroverted	Selects own goals
Moderately strong need for power, achievement	Needs little encouragement
Low inhibition	Discomfort when making decisions when there exist no organizational ground-rules
Moderate affiliation	Needs recognition
Freedom from anxiety	Is an "opinion-leader"
Strong interpersonal trust	Stimulates ambitions of associates, presents superiors with unsolicited recommendations

lenges, the active creating of challenges, an overall orientation toward activity, and a propensity for using interpersonal skills based on an expectancy of success. Rational man seeks the attainment of organizationally defined rather than personally satisfying needs and goals. He enjoys competition, can be persuasive, and uses his winning combination (or proven formula for success) in his goal-selection process. His goals are auspicious, self-selected, and beyond (or "higher" than) his present condition. Above all, this leader is a utilitarian who prefers rationality to impulsivity.

Our portrait of this leader has caused us to reexamine our original hypothesis about the personality of the activistic organizational leader. It has shown that anxiety alone is not a sufficient cause of initiative-taking behavior. We may now ask: What are some of the other psychological determinants of initiative-taking behavior, and what kinds of personality attributes are characteristic of other kinds of leaders? Let us turn to our next type of leader, the existential man, and see why he takes initiatives. Perhaps this will allow us to examine in more detail how type-specific character structures lead to differing experiences and views of the world and, ultimately, to differing leadership styles.

NOTES

1. MacDonald (1973), in his review of the literature, has maintained that "all of the research points to the same conclusion: people are handicapped by external locus of control orientations." Lefcourt (1972), however, has said that there is only an "assumed link" between perceptions of control and achievement, and Joe (1971), in reviewing several studies, has said: "Since all the scales employed in the (reviewed) studies are self-reported measures, the research suggests that externals *describe* themselves as more concerned with fear of failure than with achievement per se. Internals on the other hand, *describe* themselves as more concerned with achievement" (emphasis added).

2. While introversion-extroversion is perhaps the most stable and conceptually valid of all known personality constructs (Robinson and Shaver, 1973), its relationship to leadership behavior is unclear. Mann (1959), after reviewing 22 studies of introversion-extroversion and leadership performance in small groups, found a median correlation of .15 and concluded that "those individuals who tend to be selected as leaders are more sociable and outgoing, although the process of inferring such a characterization is tenuous at best." Extroversion characterizes but two of our four leadership types, the rational man and the existential man. Dominance, activity-passivity, and introversion-extroversion were all measured in this study by use of semantic differentials.

3. Following the factor analytic research of Mirels (1970) and Reid and Ware (1973), Rotter's fate-control scale was disaggregated and treated as containing two separable dimensions. The two dimensions measure "personal control" and "system control." Not a single rational man scored "externally" on any of the system control items. A discussion of the two dimensions is contained in Chapter 4, footnote 2.

4. Scoring of the protocols was done by an independent contractor using the Winter (1973) scoring system. Scoring reliability levels are .87. See Appendix III for a more complete discussion of the TAT methodology used in this work.

5. Formally measured through analysis of TATs, this fear of other powerful people is often referred to simply as "fear of power." The fear of power concept was developed by David Winter. For a discussion of the concept's measurement properties the interested reader should see *The Power Motive* (Winter, 1973).

6. The author wishes to thank David Winter, Ann Litwin, and McBur and Company for making the comparative data available.

7. Rational man scores higher in the need for achievement than does either the whole business or military population (two-tailed t test; t = 1.82, p < .07). His experience of personal control and his need for achievement have a Pearson correlation of .35, p < .03.

8. Harold Lasswell (1930, 1948) has long maintained that positive self-regard lessens the need to express power. Our findings seem to support his contention. For rational man the need for achievement and the need for power have an r of −.47, p < .004. Self-esteem and the need for power have an r of −.23 (NS).

9. "Activity-passivity" was measured through use of a semantic differential. For the rational man and the business population, the mean difference (two-tailed t test) was significant at the .12 level (t = 1.55), while for the military it was .001 (t = 3.41).

10. In this study we asked each participant the same opinion leadership questions that have been utilized over the years by the Survey Research Center at the University of Michigan. Forty-eight percent have tried to convince others of their political beliefs.

11. As measured through analysis of the TATs, rational men score moderately low in the "need for personal power." T tests of means between rational men and the whole business and military elites are not statistically significant.

12. For rational man self-esteem and reported frequency of creating challenges have an r of .14. Internal control and challenge seeking have an r of .10. The sense of internal control and frequency of stimulating the ambitions of associates have a Pearson correlation of .36 (p < .01), and internal control and the need for achievement have an r of .35 (p < .03).

13. Differences in the propensity to create challenges appear less than dramatic, although they are statistically significant. As this study seeks to demonstrate the validity of the leadership typology (presented in Chapter 2), what is most crucial is that we demonstrate differences in character type and the behavior that each type suggests. In the following three chapters we will be making comparisons between the four leadership types, and through these comparisons our findings will take on added (comparative) meaning. Challenge seeking is a case in point.

14. All respondents were asked, "When you are required to direct the activities of others, how often do you receive their personal respect?" Over 79 percent of the rational men answered, "always" or "very often." This was a greater percentage than answered positively among the other leadership types and once again demonstrates his positive self-regard.

15. Over 64 percent of our rational men enjoy new problems because the accomplishment gives them great pleasure; 19 percent enjoy the problem for its own sake; and only 11 percent enjoy new problems for prestige purposes.

16. McClelland and Steele (1973) have shown that high need achievers are conservative risk takers. Our evidence here supports their findings.

17. A strong relationship is found between the rational man's sense of self as a "success" and the perception of his existence as personally meaningful (r = .37, p < .007). For the business and military populations as a whole, the correlation was neither strong nor statistically significant.

18. This very point was most dramatically stated at a recent conference attended by the author. Kenneth Fisher, president and chief executive officer of Prime Computer (a newly emergent high-technology "glamor" company) stated, "if Prime was operated under the principles of logic, it would have failed five years ago." (Speech given at the Wang Institute, Tyngsboro, Massachusetts, March 16, 1981).

19. This ability to differentiate is much akin to Rokeach's (1960) conception of the "open

mind." Rokeach maintains that open-minded people do not see things in black or white, but in finer shades of grey. Such people display what Rokeach calls a healthy, "proximity between belief and disbelief systems."

CHAPTER 4

EXISTENTIAL MAN

The existential experience of being controlled by forces outside the self, coupled with high self-esteem, provides a unique perceptual frame of reference by which others are viewed and a set of principles by which all incoming information is received and catalogued.

Psychodynamically, the rational man and the existential man offer not only a quantitative contrast in like personality attributes or characteristics but a qualitative contrast in whole cognitive systems and thus fundamental world views. They offer a contrast in internal states of mind. While the rational man views the world and the manifold problems with which he is faced as reducible to comprehension through prolonged rational activity, the existential man experiences a world composed of irrational social forces. Because the existential man accepts and uses as a given the essential incomprehensibility (or uncontrollability) of the forces that shape his life, his behavior is not wholly "rational." Rather, the existential man is visceral. The preoccupation with activity in the face of uncertainty is the essential paradox of existential man and the subject of this chapter.

THE EXISTENTIAL SENSE OF SELF

Like rational man, existential man thinks much of himself and his capabilities. For example, when asked to estimate their own IQs, existential men score higher than all other leadership types.[1] Both rational and existential leaders experience a healthy coincidence between their aspirations and achievements, but the aspirations of the existential man are tempered by the interactive effects of an external sense of control. While the rational man envisions a world that offers an unlimited number of challenges, the existential man perceives the world as much more finite in its challenge-laden offerings. The existential man views himself as not less efficacious or capable but as less omnipotent. Outcomes for this leader are not always the result of personal ambition, but of the uncontrollable outside forces that exercise their power over the individual.

Let us cite a few outstanding examples of the contrasting ways in which rational and existential men experience the world: All respondents were asked to agree or disagree with the three questionnaire items presented in Table 4.1. Unlike the rational man, who dwells in a world reducible to understanding, the existential man experiences what some philosophers have called the "absurd":

> The absurd is a confrontation between the individual and his world. It is not the world which is absurd, nor is it man. The absurd is the lack of correspondence between the two. It is an *anxious* consciousness of the

Table 4.1.: Responses to Three Questions Which Seek to Measure the Degree to Which Existential and Rational Men Experience Control

Group	"Many times I feel that I have little influence over the things that happen to me" (%)		
	N	Agree	Disagree
Existential Man	22	27.3	72.7
Rational Man	41	2.3	97.7

$X^2 = 8.94$, p $<$ .005.-

Group	"Without the right breaks one cannot become an effective leader" (%)		
	N	Agree	Disagree
Existential Man	22	18.2	81.8
Rational Man	41	2.3	97.7

$X^2 = 4.85$, p $<$ .03.

Group	"Most people don't recognize the extent to which their lives are controlled by accidental happenings" (%)		
	N	Agree	Disagree
Existential Man	22	90.9	9.1
Rational Man	41	27.9	72.1

$X^2 = 2.75$, p $<$ .09.

divorce between the individual and his world. The individual is not absurd; he simply is what he is in his longing for clarity, for a meaningful response to his existence. The world is not absurd; it is what it is in its irrationality, in its ultimate lack of unity and coherency. (Existential) man and his world are what they are each in its own right; one cannot be ignored or reduced to the reality of the other, and in this confrontation of two realities the absurd emerges as the divorce which exists between these two. (Hanna, 1978: 353) (emphasis supplied)

This leader is especially sensitive to the seeming incongruence between his intentions and outcomes. He never underestimates the role of fortune or misfortune. Not only do 91 percent of the existential men believe that people "don't realize the extent to which their lives are controlled by accidental happenings," but existential men often feel they are captives of circumstance, "victims of forces they can neither control nor understand" (see Table 4.2).

How does the existential sense of being controlled by outside forces affect the elevated sense of confidence experienced by this leader? Shouldn't the perception of exogenous control lessen his self-confidence and interfere with his ability to impact his environment? While this seems to be the case for most organizational leaders,* it does not appear to be necessarily so among the existential men. For these leaders self-esteem and the sense of being controlled by external forces have a strong positive relationship indicating that the existential sense of self-esteem is positively associated with the perception of incomplete control. In other words, for the existential man positive self-regard and feelings of self confidence do not produce a belief in the ability to control organizational processes and outcomes (see Table 4.3).

The existential man does, however, attempt to exercise influence over his environment, even knowing that his efforts may not be effective in shaping important outcomes.[2] Uncertainty or anxiety concerning the effectiveness of his control renders an interesting and idiosyncratic leadership style that influences frequent use of interpersonal influence tactics aimed at strengthening the perceived improbability of effective, total control.

While we must postpone our examination of the interaction between the existential man's sense of self-esteem and his motives, the kinds of stories he writes in response to TATs illustrates the nature of the relationship between his high self-esteem and his experience of external control. Let us cite one example of a story written by an existential executive in response to the picture that we call "Two Women in Lab" (see Figure 4.1):

---

*For the whole business and military elite, self-esteem and locus of control have a Pearson correlation of $-.28$, $p < .01$.

A laboratory director had given a task to one of her technicians and the technician, after embarking, encountered a point of *uncertainty* and called the director over for assistance. The director is demonstrating an approach to resolving the *uncertainty*. The director is *confident*, yet careful

Table 4.2: **"As far as world affairs are concerned, most of us are the victims of forces we can neither control nor understand" (%)**

Group	N	Agree	Disagree
Existential Man	22	45.5	54.5
Rational Man	41	0.0	100.0

$X^2 = 22.15$, p $<$ .001.

Figure 4.1: **"Two Women in Lab"***

Just look at the picture briefly (10–15 seconds), turn the page and write out the story it suggests.

*Source: J. Veroff and S. Feld, *Marriage and Work in America*, 1970. Reprinted by permission of the senior author.

Table 4.3: Existential Man: His Levels of Self-Esteem and Locus of Control*

Group	Self-Esteem				Locus of Control			
	N	$\bar{X}$	t	p value	N	$\bar{X}$	t	p value
1. Existential Man	22	83.99 (SD = 3.57)			22	11.50 (SD = 1.50)		
2. Rational Man	43	84.91 (SD = 3.10)		NS	43	4.09 (SD = 1.52)		.001
3. Whole Business Elite	62	70.69 (SD = 10.24)		.001	60	8.00 (SD = 3.60)		.001
4. Whole Military Elite	242	72.67 (SD = 9.90)		.001	217	8.03 (SD = 3.86)		.001

*All t tests of means involving three or more groups were computed using the same procedures. Using the above table as an example, the procedures were as follows:

(1) Group 1 (Existential Man) is compared with Group 2 (Rational Man).

(2) Group 1 is compared with Group 3 (Whole Business Elite). Group 3 contains all business respondents with the exception of those who are members of Group 1, the subject population.

(3) Group 1 is compared with Group 4 (Whole Military Elite). Group 4 contains all military respondents with the exception of those who are members of Group 1, the subject population.

(4) Group 2 is then compared with Group 3. Group 3 in this t test contains all respondents except those who are members of Group 2.

(5) Group 2 is compared with Group 4. Group 4 contains all respondents except those who are members of Group 2.

These procedures allow us to compare subject populations (specific leadership types) with the parent populations from which they were drawn, minus the subject populations. In comparing a subsample to the parent population, members of the subsample must be extracted, or one would be comparing a subsample to a larger group containing members of that subsample.

To determine the total N for these types of analyses, one would add only the subject group (here Existential Man) with the two parent populations. Thus, the total N for self-esteem in Table 4.3 would be 22 + 62 + 242, or 326. The 43 rational men are "returned to" the parent populations for the existential to business elite, and the existential to military elite t tests. These principles apply throughout the book to all other analyses that compare multiple subgroups to parent populations.

Analysis of variance would appear to be far more economical than five separate t tests (indeed, it involves considerably less work). In comparing our types, however, we are not only trying to demonstrate the existence of gross differences, but specific differences *between* specific types. Blalock (1972: 328–329) comments, "The advantage of analysis of variance is that a single test may be used in place of many . . . . It should not be concluded that analysis of variance is always preferable to a series of difference-of-means tests, however. The latter tests, when used cautiously, may yield considerably more information . . . especially if one suspects *before* making the test that one or more categories will differ considerably from the others . . . ." This is precisely the situation that exists with our leadership types. Several characteristic differences were hypothesized a priori, on the basis of the typology itself.

about her procedure. The technician is *also confident* of her own work and ability, but is listening to the director she had sought. The technician resumes her work and, using the new approach, completes her task. (italics added)

Note the explicit confrontation between uncertainty and self-confidence.[3] Other stories written by existential men contain the same dialectic—positive self-regard as against a vision of an uncertain world. The reconciliation of this uncertainty by purposive action is the central paradox of existential man.

MOTIVATIONAL DETERMINANTS

The Need for Power

The existential man expresses an extremely high need for power, whether compared with other elites who took part in this study or to various groups who have been tested in the population at large.[4] This need for power is perhaps the most potent force in the character of existential man, and it informs all aspects of his leadership style. It permeates superior-subordinate relations, the handling of formal power, the taking of risks and initiatives, strategies employed for getting ahead, problem-solving modes, and the general style by which the existential man attempts to relate to others whether at work or at play.[5]

What exactly is meant by the need for power? Does it mean that an individual wishes he had power? Does it mean that he likes to influence other people? Do people with a strong need for power come to occupy formal positions of power and status? Are they attracted to powerful, high-status positions, or are they motivated to exercise influence solely because it is demanded by their formal organizational stature?

"The status of having power," states Winter (1973: 19), "is the goal of the (power) motive." A person's formal power status, and his expressed need for power as a "motive," are different concepts. Whether an individual with a high need for power brings with him that need into high-status positions, or whether that need has been "socialized" through the acquisition of high status is still uncertain. The literature suggests, however, that the power motive is fostered long before the attainment of formal positions of power. As such, it is thought to precede the acquisition of formal power positions.

The power motive may be broken down to include "hope of power" and "fear of power," distinct constructs measurable in thematic apperception. Hope of power represents the unconscious expression of a strong desire for high status. Fear of power is the expression that power may be harmful (either the power one has or the power that another may exercise over the individual). Both measures are important for understanding the nature of the strivings for power exhibited by business and military leaders. A distinction between hope for power and fear of power allows us to state why the power motive is expressed—out of hope for its attainment or out of fear of its harmful effects. Some people exert influence over other people because they want to control and impress others, and some people exert influence for fear of being controlled.[6]

A strong need for power represents a state of readiness, a propensity to act in a certain way, if given the opportunity, to express that propensity. The need for power is thus distinct from the actual expression of power tactics.

What makes a particular action or outcome attractive to a person high in the need for power is the amount of power that he gains, feels, or displays in that outcome. "In general," states Winter (1973: 204), "two things contribute to the amount of power one feels: the domain, or the number of people over whom one has power, and the range, or the set of behaviors which one can cause in these people."

Some of the more important behavior that other research has found to correlate highly with the power motive are presented in Table 4.4. People who exhibit a high need for power (as measured through thematic apperception) often attempt to impress others. When taking part in group discussions they are very expressive and attempt to be influential. When placed in a potentially competitive situation, the individual high in need for power will often become aggressive and attempt to control others' actions and decisions. People high in the need for power often nurture relationships for specific and personally rewarding reasons. They do not often express a genuine concern for other people. When given the opportunity to take risks, people with strong power needs have been found to seek impact through bold attempts at securing large, rather impressive (and often improbable) payoffs. Such persons display an unusual concern for their reputation (so they may be viewed by others as being "powerful"), they enjoy being able to "call their own shots" with regard to career paths, they often hold offices in organizations, and they are unusually concerned with acquiring prestige possessions, symbolic of their stature.

Evidence accumulated through the observation of small groups has further illustrated that people high in need for power often display actions that draw attention and attract followers. Such people have been found to gain positions of social influence. Sociometrically, these individuals are viewed as highly ego-involved and influential. Excessive power motivation, however, especially without affiliative concerns, may lead them to

Table 4.4: Behavioral Correlates of the Power Motive

The seeking of impact	Distorting information (information control)
The seeking of high visibility	Unusual concern with personal reputation
Expressive modes of participation (in small groups)	Desire for autonomy or personal control (especially with regard to career)
Capacity to form alliances when problem-solving	Holding offices in organizations
Interpersonal competitiveness	Acquiring prestige: having credit cards, driving highly maneuverable (sports) cars, etc.
The nurturance of interpersonal relationships for instrumental gain	Watching sports and reading vicarious "power" magazines (e.g., *Playboy*, *Sports Illustrated*, etc.)
Interpersonal aggressiveness	A preference for unassertive, dependent wives
The attraction to large payoffs when risk-taking	Verbal hostility
Unusual concern for maintaining influence over others	

Fear of Power	*Hope of Power*
Preference for independence or autonomy	Minimal interpersonal competitiveness
Fear of structure (especially when imposed by powerful others)	High level of organizational participation
General state of physiological arousal (general activation or stress as measured by Thayer, 1967)	More participation in less directly competitive sports (sports involving man against himself or the clock)
Stress during gaming behaviors	More acquisition of prestige objects
	Consumption of alcoholic beverages to enliven power fantasies
	A general feeling of being strong and powerful (as measured by a semantic differential)

become too highly structured and too preoccupied with intensified efforts to control. These efforts inhibit effective leadership in the small-group setting.

The following explanation has been offered by Winter (1973: 156) as to why some people fear power:

Fear of power seems to result from a reversal in the Oedipal stage. Here the boy identifies with his mother and becomes thereby a sexual object for the father (Freud, 1921). In other words, at the level of fantasy, the boy has submitted to his father, perhaps taking him as a love object. Such an impulse, either overtly or symbolically homosexual, arouses *anxiety* at a later age, and is therefore repressed. What we observe as fear of power in an adult male would thus be an *anxious* concern about power which is based on an earlier association of power with (possibly homosexual) submission . . . It is still not clear whether power or homosexuality is primary (Ovesey, 1955). (emphasis supplied)

Other, perhaps more tenable explanations may be offered. For example, fear of power as being the manifestation of other childhood and adult experiences such as living in a punitive environment (perhaps in the presence of a strong and imposing father), or actual failure of acomplishment resulting in continued fear of failure (or power imposed on the self by others), or fear of success (power attained at the expense of others). It remains unclear whether homosexuality has anything at all to do with the fear of power. In any case, fear of power, as a distinctly measurable component of the power motive, is associated with a strong preference for autonomy and the avoidance of other powerful people.

While Winter has not speculated as to the antecendents of a strong "hope of power," its behavioral attributes have been included in Table 4.4.

Other Motivational Determinants Figure Prominantly in Existential Man's Leadership Style

Though existential man expresses a strong need for power, he also has other motives that are measurable through thematic apperception. He is quite low in his need to achieve, he is extremely low in his need to affiliate with others, and he is uninhibited.

The rational and existential leaders share a number of important attributes. Neither has a strong hope of power or fear of power, though the existential man fears other powerful people more than the rational man. Of special significance is the fact that both of these leaders are essentially uninhibited (see Table 4.5).

The relatively weak need to achieve (by comparative intra-elite standards) indicates that the existential man is not preoccupied with entrepreneurial activity. He is, in all probability, not strongly drawn toward the acquisition of wealth (though he is drawn toward the acquisition of other forms of prestige). Similarly, he is not likely to be strongly concerned with creating practical innovations or whole new enterprises (behavioral correlates of the very high need achiever).[7] Successful organizational leaders need not be classic need achievers. Organi-

Table 4.5: Existential Man: His Need for Power and Affiliation and His Level of Inhibition

Group	Need Power			Need Affiliation			Inhibition		
	N	X̄	SD	N	X̄	SD	N	X̄	SD
1. Existential Man	14	4.10	4.31	14	2.11	2.45	14	.88	1.79
2. Rational Man	37	2.78	3.95	38	5.65	15.83	37	1.07	2.09
3. Whole Business Elite	53	3.43	3.98	53	3.30	2.08	52	1.43[c]	2.80
4. Whole Military Elite	175	2.78[a]	3.34	202	5.13[b]	12.58	180	1.12	1.78

[a] $t = 1.11$, $p < .28$.

[b] $t = -2.61$, $p < .01$.

[c] $t = -1.68$, $p. < .11$.

zational leadership emphasizes norms and role models rather than the creation of new enterprises.

The rather weak need to affiliate with others expressed by the existential man strongly suggests leanings toward a desire for personal autonomy. Individuals low in the need for affiliation do not experience a special propensity "to be part of a larger social setting," nor do they readily yield to the desires of others, being generally resistant to social influence (this is consonant with this leader's very high level of self-esteem, which in turn predicts a general resistance to persuasion). And, consistent with the existential man's propensity to utilize power tactics, his rather low need to affiliate with others indicates he will not easily become emotionally involved with other people.

Less than any of the other leadership types does the existential man display "activity inhibition." While the inhibited leader often envisions negative anticipations concerning the consequences of powerful action, uninhibited leaders are impulsive and expansive in their fantasies of power. That the existential man is both high in his need for power and low in his need for affiliation, as well as uninhibited, lends further credence to our portrayal of him as one whose general traits of action are influenced by a "command identity."

As he is high in self-esteem and in the need for power, he is active; as he believes his fate is controlled or otherwise determined by extrinsic forces, he is uncertain; as he is uninhibited, he is highly expressive and apt to live out his private strivings for power.

SUPERIOR-SUBORDINATE RELATIONS

When belief in the capacity to master the environment exists, one becomes confident that success will be attained. When an individual believes decisive events in his life are influenced or determined by extrinsic forces, success is not expected, for the element of chance can always work against man's best designs. As Machiavelli has exhorted, "fortuna" cannot be understood—"she" must be beaten.

In order to combat the uncertainty and irrationality of a world controlled by chance, the existential man seeks to impose structure. By placing boundaries on all work situations, by making it clear to subordinates what their roles shall be, by imposing control over his own life space and that of others, by forcing order upon chaos, the existential man hopes to limit the opportunity for the unforeseeable to rear "her" fickle head.

In order to combat the effects of chance, the existential man closely follows the course of his desired outcomes all the way to their conclusion.

Because he must closely follow the course of all that is important to him, the existential man has a strong desire for structure and feels most comfortable in an ordered work milieu.

Existential man continuously strives for the elusive control that he believes escapes him and seeks to initiate structure for his associates, whose otherwise successful achievements would invalidate his external sense of the world. A strong need for power is the psychological precondition for his "command identity," and utilization of influence tactics ensures him of an enhanced experience of control. The interaction of this leader's character and world view gives us a special glimpse of how unconscious motivations can affect practical conduct in everyday life.

While the first type of leader, the rational man, was portrayed as both trusting and trustworthy, the second type, the existential man, remains skeptical not only about his own sense of control but of the sense of control held by others. Because he doubts the ability of any man to have mastery over an irrational environment, he is never certain that the tasks that subordinates and superiors undertake will be successfully accomplished. The existential man therefore closely supervises his subordinates and attempts to control the nature of their work through the imposition of structure (see Table 4.6).The existential man believes that in the absence of clear directives subordinates fail to accomplish successfully the tasks required of them.[8] The skepticism inherent in one who experiences an external sense of control and a highly elevated sense of self-esteem produces an orientation of relative mistrust. Only the entrepreneur mistrusts his colleagues more than the existential man.

Table 4.6: Existential Man: His Feelings About Directive Leadership

Group	N	"A good leader expects people to decide for themselves what they should do" (%)	
		Agree	Disagree
Existential Man	22	2.3	97.6
Rational Man	43	22.8	77.2

Group	N	"A good leader makes it clear to everyone what his job is."(%)	
		Agree	Disagree
Existential Man	22	97.7	2.4
Rational Man	43	77.2	22.8

$X^2 = 8.14$, p $<$ .005.

Consistent with the personality attributes analyzed in the foregoing sections, the existential man assumes a commanding posture over the subordinates in whom he places relatively little trust and of whom he is highly uncertain. Not only is this leader power-oriented and in need of control, but as our semantic-differential measures indicate, he is both "domineering" and "persuasive." Our projective measures lend additional credence to this assertion. Content analysis of all TAT protocols shows that existential men depict characters who exert influence attempts or use force to get their own way between two and three times as often as do the other leadership types. (A content analysis of TATs completed by our four groups of leaders appears as Appendix IV.)

The impending sense of uncertainty and the power-dominant, low affiliation motivational field defines and delimits the way in which the existential man relates to others. While we have no direct evidence that this leader attempts to control and initiate structure through the manipulation of power symbols (use of "classified" memos, specialized access to information, etc.), Winter does provide us with evidence that such a person may attempt to control the dissemination of information within the organizational network. Information control (or distortion) has particular relevance in the military organization where certain types of information are "classified" and generally not available to subordinates.

THE EXISTENTIAL MAN AS SELF-STARTER

Taking Initiatives as a Strategy to Gain Influence

The lack of control experienced by existential man creates psychic tension or uneasiness[9] and promotes a unique, commanding style of action. Because the existential man views his colleagues as potential rivals, we would predict that he would rarely lend them his support or encourage them to get ahead in the organization. The leader who is fearful of the power of his associates would surely not stimulate their ambitions. Our evidence, however, does not support our prediction. The existential man reports that he both tries to stimulate the ambitions of his associates (95.5 percent report doing so "very often" or "often") and frequently presents his superiors with unsolicited recommendations.[10] Although the rational men display these kinds of self-starter behaviors, they do so for instrumental reasons and especially for the facilitation of group (or organizational) goals. The existential man takes initiatives both as a strategy to gain influence and as a way of gaining personal control.

From the evidence presented thus far it is unclear whether (as we claim) the existential man stimulates the ambitions of his associates and frequently presents them with unsolicited recommendations as a form of influence-building, or whether, for example, such behavior results from a sense of obligation to the organization. The existential man expresses a moderately strong sense of obligation to the job (over 63 percent "strongly agree" that "it is the duty of each person to do his job the very best he can"), and he feels quite strongly that life becomes meaningful "only when one devotes oneself to an ideal or a cause" (19 percent "strongly agreed" with that statement, while another 62 percent "agreed").

One possible interpretation of these data is that the existential man presents recommendations and attempts to stimulate the ambition of his associates out of a sense of duty, perhaps deriving from the ethos of his particular organization. But let us review the existential character: He is preoccupied with strivings for power and is unusually concerned with maintaining his position of influence. The imagery he projects via the TAT indicates he is more concerned with the larger group than with himself. He has very little trust in his superiors (with whom he rubs elbows daily), yet he reports a strong sense of "duty" to (the more psychologically remote) organization. He rarely needs to socialize with his associates (nor does he seek nurturance from them), yet he believes that it is only when he devotes himself to an "ideal" or a "cause" that his life becomes meaningful.

A very interesting picture emerges of the existential sense of hierarchic space.[11] As reconstructed from our data, Figure 4.2 illustrates how the existential man views the organization as above himself and above the organization's human parts. Subconsciously, the existential man views the organization and its human members as discrete phenomena. Spatially, he views the organization as "higher" than its leaders (in whom he places comparatively little trust) and above himself. It need not matter that these leaders actually direct the organization and help to make it what it is. His superiors are proximate, animate objects. They are "real" objects toward which he may direct his uncertainty and disquietude. The "organization," "ideal," "duty," and "cause" are separate and above the workaday world of the busy leader. They are more distant phenomena, above human relations, and of a quality clearly superior to and different from their human components. While the existential man can never be sure of his future or the actions of his superiors and subordinates, he can be certain of the organization, the one constant in a psychic world strongly influenced by external forces.

Robert Presthus (1962: 156) has also noted the way in which members of large bureaucracies differentiate between the organization and organizational men:

> Big organizations often become a psychic reality, reflecting our tendency
> to reify abstractions such as the "church" or the "nation." ... When the

Figure 4.2: Existential Man and His Sense of Hierarchic Space

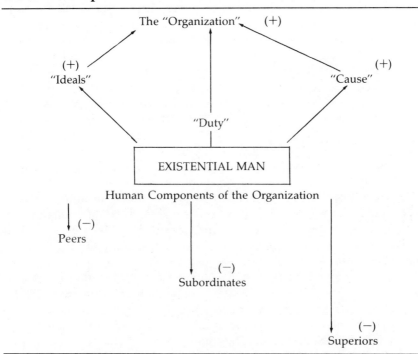

retiring clerk says, "the corporation has been good to me," we may suppose that he actually thinks of the "corporation" as an entity distinct from those who represent it. The significance of such myths, of course, is not that they are illogical but that they influence behavior.

We have strayed some from the theme that the existential man presents superiors with unsolicited recommendations and stimulates the ambitions of his associates in order to enlarge his organizational sphere of influence. Let us return to our examination and see if other forms of initiative taking constitute for existential man a strategy to get ahead.

Challenge Seeking

Frequent challenge seeking is a salient characteristic not only of leadership style but of a general strategy for acquiring prestige and status. Of course, if the challenges being sought are not successfully met, a loss in prestige may occur. In the case of the existential man, challenge-seeking is an attempt to gain control. Risk of failure is never even considered.

The locus of control literature would predict that externally oriented people are not seekers of challenges. Yet our data indicate that they may be, if the (external) perception of control is accompanied by strong self-confidence. Table 4.7 shows that despite his belief that external forces may determine his fate, the existential man seeks challenges well above the norm for all the elites. (And we should again bear in mind that our sample populations are composed largely of initiative takers.) Upon close inspection of Table 4.7 the reader will notice that the existential man, more than even the rational man, reports he actively seeks challenges "always" or "very often" (81.8 percent vs. 72.1 percent). Table 4.8 also shows that existential men create challenges significantly more than their colleagues.

What is perhaps most striking about the comparative data presented thus far is not the difference in frequency and kind of initiative-taking behavior displayed by rational and existential men but the similarity. The rational man is highly "internal" and anxiety-free; the existential man highly "external" and imbued with anxiety. How is it that they both take initiatives? Doesn't the existential experience of being controlled by outside forces foster a fatalistic and quietistic approach to life? Not so. Think of Sisyphus, Camus' (1955) existential hero. His life was dedicated to rolling a boulder up a mountain, even knowing that the boulder was destined to roll back down. The effort, not the accomplishment of that effort, was the essence of Sisyphus' life.

The rational man, as we have suggested, is a utilitarian. He takes initiatives because by doing so he does his job better. The outcomes of his initiative-taking behavior are what make him happy. Not coincidentally, these outcomes enhance his position in the organization. The rational man does not need to seek challenges—he does so because he wants to.

The meaning of challenge-seeking behavior is quite different for the existential man. More than any other leadership type the existential man feels a need to actively seek out new challenges. His actions derive from a strong need to control processes and outcomes that are seemingly irrational yet important to him. His motivation for control is strong and is informed by a need for power. The uncertainty inextricably bound up with the experience that forces outside of him control his fate produces a need to impose structure or a need to impose order where there is chaos. It is only through the imposition of structure that this type of leader may hope to control outcomes and reduce the anxiety that emanates from his experience of a disordered world. The experience of being controlled by exogenous forces, when accompanied by a lack of inhibition, produces an active orientation toward the world and a need to bring it under reign. It is his essentially uninhibited character that allows him to act out his personal

Table 4.7: "About how often do you actively seek challenges?" (%)

Group	N	Always	Very Often	Often	Not Very Often
1. Existential Man	22	18.1	63.6	18.1	0.0
2. Rational Man	43	25.6	46.5	23.3	4.6
3. Whole Business Elite	62	7.0	56.1	33.3	3.5
4. Whole Military Elite	242	3.8	34.3	41.9	20.0

$X^2 = 2.35$, NS (Groups 1 and 2).
$X^2 = 31.01$, p. $< .001$ (Groups 1, 3, and 4).

71

Table 4.8: Source of Challenge-Seeking Among Existential Men

"Would you consider yourself a person who *actively* looks for challenges, or someone who becomes motivated primarily through challenges that appear on your desk?" (%)

Group	N	(Self) Actively Look	(Environment) Respond to Challenges Presented
1. Existential Man	22	90.9	9.0
2. Rational Man	43	86.0	9.3
3. Whole Business Elite	62	77.2	21.1
4. Whole Military Elite	242	68.1	30.0

$X^2 = .007$, NS (Groups 1 and 2).
$X^2 = 5.78$, p. $< .06$ (Groups 1, 3, and 4).

need for control and to externalize rather than repress that need. This finding is consistent with the literature that suggests that anxiety can be a spur to positive forms of action.[12]

Our data suggest that it is precisely because of the uncertainty generated by incomplete control that action is taken. Whether the motives behind the actions are selfish or altruistic depends on several other interrelated personality factors, such as the need for personal and social power, and an equally important host of situational factors, such as the opportunity for expression of personal needs. This is not to say that insecurity (or uncertainty) is a necessary or even sufficient cause for the taking of initiatives. It certainly need not, however, inhibit such behavior.

The form and extent of initiative-taking behavior differ among the various leadership types because the interpretation of important events and the world view itself are different. The meaning of the challenge is different. A secure man, comfortable with his sense of achievement and believing in his ability to control outcomes that are important to him, will often act because he is free to express both his curiosity and his intentions. In the organizational context, this man will not fear adverse reactions from his superiors. The man who is uncertain either of his ability to achieve or his ability to control may act to validate his sense of self to compensate for perceived inadequacy or merely to improve a current condition that he finds unsatisfying. Yet he *does* act.[13]

At this juncture I would like to suggest that only when one is able to externalize private needs can the expression of private motives in public conduct be paramount. Only then can private motives replace the imperative of organizational norms.

There is a great difference in the behavior of the leader who lacks control and wants it and the leader who lacks control and thinks he can never get it. It is inhibition that plays a central role here. The leader who lacks control but is uninhibited wants control and tries to get it. The leader who experiences external control and is inhibited accepts his "other-directedness" and copes with his anxiety in other (more private) ways.

THE EXISTENTIAL MAN AND SITUATIONAL AMBIGUITY

Thus far we have seen that the existential man displays a number of self-starter characteristics: He is highly active (as measured by semantic differential), he very often attempts to stimulate the ambition of his associates, he often presents superiors with unsolicited recommendations, he is a frequent seeker of challenges, and he attempts to create challenges more often than any other leadership type.

Where there are no clear guidelines to action, no precedents or ground rules by which to frame judgments and hence to make decisions, taking action is particularly difficult. In fact, many leaders are excellent "game players" or norm enforcers, yet they are unable to free themselves from organizational norms and make decisions for which there are no ground rules or precedents. In this context Daniel Katz (1969: 695) has said, "innovative and spontaneous activity in achieving organizational objectives which go beyond . . . role specifications, is *essential* for a functioning organization" (emphasis supplied). Yet not all leaders are able to perform this "essential" function.

Ordinarily, the leader may avail himself of one of three possible strategies in deciding how to act in the face of incomplete or altogether missing guidelines for action. First, he may seek to obtain more information. The leader may feel uncomfortable about making his decision without additional knowledge and may feel dependent on this (or a clearly delineated set of norms) for "rational" decision making. A second strategy would be to refrain from acting, for such action could be considered hasty, irrational, or chancy. Here, too, the leader may feel discomfort about being decisive in the absence of ground rules (which at least function to limit possible alternative courses of action). And third, the leader could act, in spite of his uncertainty. While the reader may think this final strategy is foolish or impetuous, there are many conditions under which a decision must be made, whether or not ground rules for that decision have been laid. For the military leaders the battlefield can be such a situation.

The theory of the self-starter outlined in Chapter 1 postulates that decisiveness in the face of uncertainty is a particular talent, not common to all men nor even all effective leaders of men. While the organizational man transposes extant norms into action, the self-starter initiates action upon which future norms are based. The self-starter is thus able to function effectively without guidance from the existing normative system. He is able to formulate courses of action by direction from within.[14]

Existential man is visceral; his mien domineering, his identity "commanding," take charge. His motivations, of course, may not always be constructive or his goals congruent with those of his organization. But by all available indicators, the existential man acts. Evidence presented in Table 4.9 indicates that he acts whether or not there are ground rules (note the feeling of discomfort displayed by rational men, leaders who are less impulsive and more reliant on "information").

We would like to suggest an interpretation of these data which is consistent with the existential view of the world and the character that informs that view.

Being faced with situational ambiguity does not present the existential man with a unique or especially challenging situation. He lives in an ambiguous world. The capacity to find order in experience is the classic

Table 4.9: "How comfortable do you feel about making decisions about which there exist no organizational ground rules, precedents?" (%)

Group	N	Very Uncomfortable/ Uncomfortable	Somewhat Uncomfortable	Not at all Uncomfortable
1. Existential Man	22	4.5	27.2	68.2
2. Rational Man	43	18.6	25.6	53.5
3. Whole Business Elite	62	15.8	43.9	40.9
4. Whole Military Elite	242	8.1	53.8	37.0

$X^2 = 2.60$, NS (Groups 1 and 2).
$X^2 = 7.89$, p. $< .08$ (Groups 1, 3 and 4).

existential coping strategy. Positive self-regard and a state of mind that accepts habitual disorder make the existential man uniquely capable of successfully dealing with new and unusual circumstances. He is a leader who is able to cope with novelty, whether or not there is a clear prescription for action. In contrast with the rational man he is visceral; action-oriented first, contemplative second. The results of the regression analysis presented in Table 4.10 support our argument. The existential experience of being controlled by outside forces contributes significantly to his unusual ability to make decisions that lack clear organizational ground rules (B = .82, p $< .001$). And this experience is forcefully buttressed by a strong will that is expressed through power tactics.

Table 4.10: Existential Man: The Relationship Between His Personality and His Ability to Make Decisions that Lack Organizational Ground Rules (N = 22)

Personality Characteristics	Regression Coefficient
Self-esteem	.05
External locus of control	.82*
Need for power	.97*
Need for achievement	.56**

$R^2 = .62$ (p. $< .02$)
F = 6.33

*p $< .001$.
**p $< .01$.

THE NEED FOR RECOGNITION

Though the existential man as self-starter needs little encouragement, he does have a strong need to be recognized for his accomplishments.[15] Over 18 percent of our existential leaders "strongly agreed" that after successfully completing a long and arduous task it was very important to them that they be recognized for their accomplishments. Over 59 percent "agreed" and only 4.5 percent "disagreed." The need for recognition (that is, the need to have impact) is consonant with, and nearly identical to, this leader's need for power.

The self-starter who needs no recognition may indeed be a great taker of initiatives or even a great innovator. Yet can such a self-starter be a great leader? I think not. Such a man would be more akin to Maccoby's "craftsman"—unconcerned with maintaining control over men or creating impact. While the existential man is driven to do, to act, and to acquire prestige, he must be recognized for his efforts. Only the technician derives pure satisfaction from the process of working on the challenge. Only the technican need not be recognized for his accomplishments.

It is characteristic of leaders that they need to create a forceful image, need to impress others, and need to bring others under their personal control. The importance of this assertion is borne out by an award-winning publication that appeared in the *Harvard Business Review* (McClelland and Burnham, 1976). Entitled "Power Is the Great Motivator," the article reported the results of a training program that endeavored to transform "average" business executives into highly motivated and dynamic leaders of men by raising their power motivation. Implicit in the construction of the program was the notion that leadership in the absence of power motivation is not leadership at all. What is interesting is that this article was judged to be of such importance that it received the *Review*'s award for the best single article published in 1976.

While the existential man as self-starter does have a relatively strong need to be recognized for his accomplishments and while he does report he is satisfied with his job,[16] this does not mean that the existential man would be content with either his job or himself if he were for some reason unable to move into a higher position of status and power within his organization. If for any reason the existential man was prevented from obtaining more status, more prestige, more power, his most dominant need system would be shut down. This type of leader needs an expansive organization, flexible enough to accommodate his expansive need for power in all its forms. Table 4.11 shows that not one existential man would be content if he were prevented from moving onward and upward. The existential man as self-starter must be able to move—to obtain more and to remain active. He must continue to impress.

Table 4.11: **"If it became apparent that you could not move into a higher position in your sponsoring organization, would you remain content with your present job?"** (%)

Group	N	Yes	No
1. Existential Man	22	0.0	100.0
2. Rational Man	41	11.6	83.7
3. Whole Business Elite	49	10.9	78.2
4. Whole Military Elite	195	10.5	82.8

$X^2 = 2.91$, p. $< .09$ Groups 1 and 2).
$X^2 = 2.86$, NS (Groups 1, 3 and 4).

THE PARADOX OF EXISTENTIAL MAN

The focus of tension, the inherent paradox of the existential man, revolves around his need to be active. While the existential man as leader and as self-starter believes that he has incomplete control of his fate, he does not diminish his level of activity or assume a quietistic posture. In no way does his perception of incomplete control inhibit the existential man from taking initiatives.

That his preoccupation with activity takes the form of a quest for certainty is not surprising. The remarkable ability of such a man, to be fully able to act in the face of uncertainty, to be able to impose order on a world conceived of as being in disorder, is the central paradox of the classic existential man. It is because of his remarkable resiliency and strength and his devotion to a cause that the existential man is not only an effective leader and a motivated self-starter but an effective leader of men.[17] Of all the leadership types in this study, the existential group contains the largest percentage (62 percent) of military officers who were promoted in an accelerated fashion.[18]

Existentials are not only men who need to act, but they are leaders who act out their needs. While the existential leader believes he can never be sure of his future successes, he strives nevertheless. And while a general sense of fate control eludes him, as a leader he functions most effectively in situations where precedent, ground rules and control are absent.

In a study done over 30 years ago, long before empirical notions of "internality" and "externality" had been developed, W. E. Henry (1949: 389) said of over 100 business executives who had taken part in a series of in-depth interviews:

> In spite of their firmness of character and their drive to activity, they also harbor a rather pervasive feeling that they may not succeed and be able to

do the things they want to do. It is not implied that this sense of frustration comes only from their immediate business experience. It seems far more likely to be a feeling of long-standing within them and to be only accentuated and reinforced by their present business experience.

It would seem more appropriate to say that the long-standing sense of uncertainty results not so much in frustration as it does in anxiety, uneasiness. This anxiety about controlling future outcomes, coupled with his belief that he is capable, distinguishes the existential man and powers an active orientation toward the world.

OVERVIEW OF THE EXISTENTIAL MAN

The existential man is a remarkably resilient leader, high in self-esteem, yet uncertain of his fate (see Table 4.12). He has been shown to have a stronger need for power than any of the other leadership types in this study. While this need for power is the distinctive mark of the existential man, and while the existential man exhibits relatively little trust in superiors and subordinates, he is a firm believer in the higher ideals of his organization.

His command identity informs all aspects of his leadership style, from the handling of power and superior subordinate relations to the taking of initiatives, which he does (with bold self-assurance) in order to enlarge

Table 4.12: Existential Man: His Character and Behavior

Character	Behavior
High self-esteem	Imposes structure
Experience of external control	Closely supervises subordinates
Domineering	Takes initiatives as strategy to gain influence
Very strong need for power, moderate need for achievement	Actively seeks challenges
Very low inhibition	Actively creates challenges
Low affiliation	Comfortable making decisions when there exist no organizational
Moderate-high anxiety	groundrules
Mistrusting	Stimulates ambitions of associates, presents superiors with unsolicited
"Command identity"	recommendations

his domain of influence. The existential man is not only an effective organizational leader or a driven self-starter; he is also a leader of men.

NOTES

1. All participants in the study were asked (through completion of a semantic differential) to estimate their IQ's. There is no reason to believe that mean differences in IQ actually exist among the leadership types.

2. It is of interest to note that among existential men, their belief in the ability to control their own actions and emotions is inversely related to their belief in the ability to control their environment ($r = -.53, p < .01$). This is highly unusual and again suggests that for this leader self-esteem is not adversely affected by the experience of incomplete control. Following the factor analytic research of Mirels (1970) and Reid and Ware (1973), the fate-control construct was treated both as a whole and as consisting of two separable dimensions: "personal control" and "system control." Personal control indicates the ability to control one's feelings, emotions, and actions. System control indicates a perceived ability to control one's environment.

3. A content analysis of all TAT protocols reveals that existential men depict characters expressing manifest uncertainty more than twice as often as the rational or administrative men.

4. One may, for example, compare the need for power scores of the existential man with those presented in Table 3.4, or with the various groups tested in McClelland et al., (1972). Again, however, when making comparisons between studies that employ the TAT, the reader is advised to interpret these comparisons with caution.

5. The existential man greatly enjoys competition not only at work but in leisure as well. Seventy-five percent report that they have participated formally in competitive sports.

6. The sense of externality or personal causation as developed by De Charms (1968) can also be distinguished from the need for power. A person who experiences fate control or internality may feel power, precisely because he believes he is the master of his fate. A strong sense of internality, however, "strongly suggests autonomy, while power seems more akin to 'control of the fate of others' " (Winter, 1973: 18). This distinction gets to the heart of the difference between locus of control and the need for power as expressed through thematic apperception. "The power motive suggests a striving toward a goal or incentive; such striving could occur in the presence as well as the absence of the goal itself" (Winter, 1973: 18).

7. Probably the most recent (and complete) review of need achievement research can be found in Fineman (1977).

8. When asked, "How often do you think that most subordinates would try to take advantage of you if they got the chance?" almost 10 percent answered, "Very often," while 23 percent answered "Often." This may be contrasted with the rational man whose responses were 4.5 and 14 percent, respectively.

9. At least eight published studies have shown that people who believe they have incomplete control are anxious. Some of the more frequently cited are Hountras and Scharf (1970) and Watson (1967).

10. Over 9 percent report doing so "always," while another 82 percent report doing so "very often" or "often." It is, of course, conceivable that existential men report that they stimulate the ambitions of their associates, even though they do not.

11. Our content analysis of all TAT protocols vividly illustrates this leader's sensitivity toward hierarchic relations. The existential man depicts characters expressing manifest concern with superior-subordinate relations about twice as often as rational and administrative men and about one-third more than the entrepreneur.

12. This is the major theme of social contract thinkers like Hobbes, who believed that the fear and anxiety of primitive society were what induced men into forming "social contracts." It also receives currency in the works of Lasswell and Weber and, more recently, Rollo May (1977). Wallace (1956: 761–764) maintains that stress especially affects people who are ambitious and will increase "primary thought processes."

13. Much has been written on the concept of self-validation, and one of the more interesting discussions (in a political context) may be found in Robert E. Lane's *Political Thinking and Consciousness* (Chapter 7), in which the author discusses the acquisition of status as a compensating behavior.

14. All bureaucratic leaders are, of course, largely bound to the norms of their respective organizations. When the opportunity arises for personal initiative taking (however frequently or infrequently), the self-starter is able to formulate his own course of action. He is not dependent on others or on a set of proscribed rules for behavior. In this sense he is an "innovator."

15. Less than 5 percent report they need encouragement "very often," while almost one-quarter (the largest percentage of all types) report they "rarely" or "never" need encouragement. This leader's need for encouragement and his experience of being controlled by exogenous forces have a Pearson correlation of $-.39$, $p < .03$. The external sense of control does not demand support from others. Rather, it encourages personal autonomy, or at times, withdrawal.

16. Almost 65 percent report they are "completely" or "very satisfied" with the amount of challenges with which they are presented while on the job, and 90 percent report they enjoy their "typical" workday.

17. Lenin was just such a man. He did not trust the determinism of orthodox Marxism—that the revolution would be the logical outgrowth of antagonisms inherent in his society. Lenin could not leave it to "history" (or the fates) to determine his outcome or the outcome of the revolution. He sought to make certain his fate through purposive revolutionary activity. Those orthodox Marxists like Karl Kautsky who refused to act on history were labeled "passive renegades." Lenin imposed structure on the revolution by a vanguard (from above) and controlled the vanguard by imposition of structure from within. He called this "discipline" (Lenin 1969). For a psychoanalytic examination of party discipline, the reader might want to see Nathan Leites, *A Study in Bolshevism* (1953), where in Chapter 5 the author develops the theme that party discipline entailed "control of feelings" and "control of spontaneity."

18. Promotion rates cover, on the average, a 12-year period.

ADMINISTRATIVE MAN

The administrative man experiences a strong sense of control. He lives in a world governed not by unknown forces or the whim of chance, but by man's capabilities and passions. Despite his belief that he is the master of his fate, this leader is insecure. His experience of personal control does not effectively enhance his sense of self-worth. This leader is anxious because he is uncertain about his ability to achieve continued success in the organization.

The administrative man is more reliant than self-reliant, more a norm enforcer than a creator of norms, and more a follower than his formal leadership status would encourage us to predict. The psychological struggle of this leader concerns his self-image.

THE ADMINISTRATOR'S SELF-IMAGE

The way in which other people regard us is central to our image of ourselves. The boldest statement of this theory was made by Charles H. Cooley (1956), who felt that the central determinant of a person's self-concept is how he thinks other people think of him—thus the famous looking-glass self. While we have stressed the notion that self-esteem is not wholly founded upon the opinions of others, the concept of the looking-glass self is important for understanding how some kinds of people behave. Administrative man is such a person. His psychological struggle centers around his perception of how he is viewed by others. The administrative man is constantly riddled with doubts about his looking-glass self. He wonders, "Do my colleagues like me . . . do they have faith in me? . . . do they respect me?" When the world looks at him, the administrative man worries about what it sees.

While he is highly oriented toward problem solving and analytic behavior, this type of leader struggles with his need to achieve. It is not so much production, per se, or the solving of difficult problems that causes the administrative man to be anxious; it is how others will receive and evaluate what he produces that causes anxiety. The task or the problem itself is less the hurdle than is the private anxiety created over public acceptance of the solution. Because he is anxious about being evaluated by others, he tries very hard to relate to people in a positive manner. He often tries too hard. His continued attempts to be liked only fail, and the administrative man is often viewed as self-centered, even egotistical (Boyatzis, 1973).

Yet the administrative man is occupationally successful. This type of leader is successful for two reasons: His personal goals are congruent with the expectations of his organization; and his organization provides the type of environment that satisfies and allows him to express his personal needs. Goal congruence provides him with a set of norms and a sense of direction that serve to minimize the natural conflict that arises when personal needs and professional expectations collide.[1]

While the organization "needs" the norm enforcer in order to maintain itself and further its own goals, the administrative man uses the environment provided him by his organization to satisfy deeply embedded needs—in particular, the prepotent need to achieve. Administrative man is akin to William Whyte's famous "organization man," yet he is less the passive instrument of the organization. The administrative man and his organization have a deeply symbiotic relationship.[2]

THE WORLD VIEW OF ADMINISTRATIVE MAN

The world view of administrative man is wrought with tension and blended with resignation. Administrative man knows he can reap great rewards if, and only if, he assimilates himself into the normative system laid before him by his organization. If he takes the organization's goals as his own, success will be his. The assimilative process involves extraordinary self-discipline and a sense of compromise. In company policymaking and political realms, the administrative man expresses reformist sentiments. He displays little of the detached instrumentalism that marks the rational man and even less the anxiety-driven boldness that characterizes the existential leader. The administrative man does not employ power tactics and strategems of manipulation in his attempts at getting ahead, for his world has no need of manipulation. His world is relatively stable, governed by clearly defined normative courses of action that provide for predictable sanctions and rewards.

Administrative man is anxious about how often and how much he should direct his achievement-related efforts toward the attainment of organizationally defined and rewarded goals. The point of uncertainty is not, as it is for the existential man, the point at which the forces of the world impinge upon the goals of the individual; but it is the point at which the individual's capabilities and sense of compromise collide with the world's expectations.

This type of leader attains success primarily because he is especially deft at translating extant policy into action. He is a leader who sustains rather than creates norms. From the view of the organization, his role as an "administrative man" is irreplaceable.

THE ADMINISTRATIVE MAN AND HIS SENSE OF SELF

When asked questions about his sense of self-worth, the administrative man consistently shows his insecurity. Though he is by all objective measures a great success, responses to the question posed in Table 5.1 indicate he does not view himself as such.[3] The administrative man, unlike the two leadership types we have already presented, suffers from a lack of self-esteem. Even though he has proved throughout his successful career that he is capable of solving most problems that come his way, he continues to doubt his professional abilities (see Tables 5.2 and 5.3).

The insecurity that this type of leader experiences derives not only from his achievement-related anxiety. Other infirmities of his self-image are apparent. Of particular significance is his fear of disapproval by others. This fear is especially strong when the administrator is in the limelight. He is especially anxious when having to speak in front of his colleagues or when making presentations (see Table 5.4).

Not only does the administrative man score consistently lower on questionnaire items that directly measure his self-esteem, but he also expresses insecurity in less direct ways. For example, when asked to rank-order a number of characteristics that contribute to his occupational success, the administrative man typically ranks self-confidence lower than do all other leadership types. Similarly, when asked how he feels when

Table 5.1: "How often do you feel you are a successful person?" (%)

Group	N	Always	Very Often	Often	Not very Often/Never
1. Administrative Man	23	0.0	17.4	56.5	26.1
2. Rational Man	43	11.6	72.1	11.6	0.0
3. Existential Man	22	36.3	45.4	18.2	0.0
4. Whole Business Elite	50	6.0	40.0	40.0	14.0
5. Whole Military Elite	192	4.7	39.6	49.5	5.2

$X^2 = 56.20$, p. $< .001$ (Groups 1, 2, and 3).
$X^2 = 17.36$, p. $< .009$ (Groups 1, 4, and 5).

Table 5.2: "How certain are you of your ability to accomplish the tasks which will be required of you in the job role(s) for which you are now training?" (%)

Group	N	Very Certain	Certain	Slightly Certain/Uncertain
1. Administrative Man	23	17.4	60.9	21.6
2. Rational Man	42	76.7	20.9	0.0
3. Existential Man	22	72.7	27.3	0.0
4. Whole Business Elite	50	45.1	43.7	10.0
5. Whole Military Elite	192	47.9	42.5	8.0

$X^2 = 30.98$, p. $< .001$ (Groups 1, 2, and 3).
$X^2 = 12.29$, p. $< .01$ (Groups 1, 4, and 5).

Table 5.3: "How often do you feel you can do everything well?" (%)

Group	N	Always	Very Often	Often	Not Very Often/Never
1. Administrative Man	23	0.0	4.3	26.1	69.6
2. Rational Man	43	9.3	69.8	16.3	2.3
3. Existential Man	22	13.6	54.5	27.2	4.5
4. Whole Business Elite	50	2.0	26.0	34.0	38.0
5. Whole Military Elite	192	3.1	22.9	41.1	31.7

$X^2 = 53.64$, p. < .001 (Groups 1, 2, and 3).
$X^2 = 14.16$, p. < .03 (Groups 1, 4, and 5).

Table 5.4: "When you talk in front of a class or a group of people your own age, how afraid or worried do you usually feel?" (%)

Groups	N	Very Worried	Worried	Slightly Worried	Not Worried at all
1. Administrative Man	23	13.0	34.8	52.0	0.0
2. Rational Man	43	0.0	0.0	30.2	69.8
3. Existential Man	22	0.0	0.0	27.3	72.7
4. Whole Business Elite	50	8.0	22.0	42.0	28.0
5. Whole Military Elite	194	2.1	9.8	60.3	27.8

$X^2 = 49.96$, p. $< .001$ (Groups 1, 2, and 3).
$X^2 = 28.75$, p. $< .001$ (Groups 1, 4, and 5).

required to direct subordinates, the administrative man most frequently reports feelings of discomfort.

THE INTERACTION OF INSECURITY AND THE PERCEPTION OF CONTROL

How does the experience of insecurity interact with his strong sense of internal control? Wouldn't it seem that belief in the ability to control one's fate would strengthen feelings of security? Would it not seem reasonable to assume that people who believe they are in control of their environment would also believe themselves to be personally efficacious?[4] For the administrative man, such is not the case. This type of leader envisages a world of order and understands the benefits of a career played by the rules of the game. Luck, fate, chance, and other exogenous forces are insignificant factors in his stab at a successful life. Personal ability and a sense of willingness to do what one must to succeed are the sole determinants of his fate.

Because the administrative man knows he can succeed if he meets the expectations of his organization, he painfully accepts all responsibility for ultimate success and failure. Unlike the existential leader, who believes his fate is controlled by forces outside him, the administrative man cannot absolve himself of his destiny. As his capabilities, his sense of willingness and ardor determine his future, it is he, and not some force extrinsic to himself, who must bear the responsibility for that future. It is this knowledge, that fate lies only in his hands, which creates the principal psychological burden of the administrative man (see Table 5.5).

When compared to other elite professionals in this study or to the population at large,[5] it is evident that this type of leader experiences a strong perception of control. Compared with either the rational man or the existential man, the administrative man is insecure. But, unlike the insecurity that marks the existential man (and that derives from his belief that he is the victim of forces he can neither control nor understand), the insecurity driving the administrative man is twofold: He is anxious about whether his personal capabilities can provide him with the means to achieve success (a state of affairs determined only by "personal causation"), and he is insecure about how others view him and his accomplishments.

How does this twofold sense of security interact with other important personality characteristics that determine leadership style? An examination of administrative man's motive dispositions should provide us with some clue.

Table 5.5: Administrative Man: His Levels of Self-Esteem and Locus of Control

Group	N	Self-Esteem			Locus of Control		
		X̄	t	p value	X̄	t	p value
1. Administrative Man	23	6.83 (SD = 4.15)			4.45 (SD = 1.11)		
2. Rational Man	43	84.91 (SD = 3.10)	23.39	.001	4.09 (SD = 1.52)	−1.10	NS
3. Existential Man	22	83.99 (SD = 3.57)	19.21	.001	11.50 (SD = 1.50)	17.77	.001
4. Whole Business Elite	63	73.02 (SD = 10.63)	−4.90	.001	8.72 (SD = 3.52)	−5.68	.001
5. Whole Military Elite	242	74.12 (SD = 9.77)	−5.97	.001	8.57 (SD = 3.82)	−5.12	.001

MOTIVATIONAL DETERMINANTS

"The Need for Achievement"—Other Investigations

Almost 20 years ago, David McClelland wondered what it was that caused cultures to rise and fall. His understanding of human motivation led him to hypothesize that the growth and decay of cultures were primarily due to the "personality" characteristics of its peoples. Specifically, it was due to the presence or absence of a peoples' achieving disposition. In search of evidence in support of his hypothesis, McClelland undertook an ambitious journey through history. By sampling traces of long-decayed cultures through examination of various artifacts, folktales and novels, McClelland hoped he could illustrate the effect of the "achieving per-sonality" on the march of history. The result of McClelland's efforts was a fascinating account of personality and culture. Entitled *The Achieving Society* (1961), McClelland's heuristic work spawned literally hundreds of investi-gations into the nature of the achievement motive.

We shall endeavor to broaden our understanding of the ways in which need achivement can affect leadership in complex organizations by briefly summarizing the dominant characteristics of the need to achieve. This has been done in Table 5.6.

The high need achiever displays energetic, innovative activity. He has been said to personify the inventiveness imparted by the "spirit of

Table 5.6: Basic Characteristics of the Need Achiever

Displays innovative, energetic activity
Engages in instrumental activity
Has a desire for *personal* feedback (need for knowledge of results of actions)
Succeeds in becoming upwardly mobile
Has a penchant for long-range planning
Is very responsive to feedback
Exhibits problem-solving mindedness
Displays moderate risk-taking behavior
Sets rational, achievable goals
Tries out new things, travels more;
    shows great interest in researching the environment

Sources of Need Achievement

Had mothers who encouraged and expected self-reliance
Had parents who placed few restrictions on the need achieving child
Had parents who encouraged the child to master something at an early age
Came from a non-punitive familial environment

capitalism"—he seeks to build a bigger and better mousetrap. The high need achiever prefers situations in which he may employ skill to the exclusion of luck or chance. He is strongly oriented toward problem-solving activities and readily desires responsibility in his place of work. The strong need achiever often displays a willingness for long-range planning and prefers taking risks of a moderate, realizable nature. He sets high goals for himself, but these goals are well within his grasp. He works hardest when the chances of succeeding are only moderately great, as such a situation stimulates his competitive edge. Finally, there is evidence that strong need for achievement is associated with upward social mobility (Crockett, 1973).

A glance at the "sources of need achievement" listed in Table 5.6 yields few surprises. Much as the socialization literature (for example, Hyman, 1959; Kahn, 1969) suggests that permissive, encouraging forms of child-rearing produce well adjusted adults, the motivation literature indicates that similar child-rearing forms encourage the nurturance of a strong need to achieve. As well, the child achiever is encouraged to master some activity at an early age, though not too early as this could cause duress. The need achieving child has been found to be relatively free from the anxiety created by excessive restrictions and/or punishments. In short, the child who most readily develops a strong need to achieve is one who is gently but firmly encouraged to master or control some form of activity at an early age. This mastery has been shown to be associated with innovative, even entrepreneurial behavior in adults.[6]

Administrative Man as a Need Achiever

Whether compared with the business and military elite of this study or with samples of corporate managers and college students tested by other researchers, the administrative man displays an extraordinarily high need for achievement (see Table 5.7). Analysis of stories written in response to our three TAT pictures illustrates that the frequency with which administrative man displays achievement motivation is three times that of the whole business elite or our matched sample of corporate managers. The administrator's penchant for achievement activity and the vigor he displays in solving problems cannot be doubted. Such a leader is dominated by the desire to produce and the desire to problem-solve for innovative change. Yet, it is paradoxical that this need, so constructive by nature, has its roots in a sense of basic insecurity.

What is the connection between insecurity, a sense of responsibility, and a strong need for achievement? Can the need for achievement, a personality disposition linked with innovation, and the rise of cultures be

Table 5.7: The Administrative Man as Need Achiever and Levels of Need Achievement Among Samples of Professional Managers and College Students

Group	N	$\bar{X}$	SD	t	p value
1. Administrative Man	16	11.08	4.21		
2. Rational Man	37	7.66	4.34	−1.34	.19
3. Existential Man	14	5.10	4.49	−1.87	.07
4. Whole Business Elite	53	3.14	3.19	3.19	.004
5. Whole Military Elite	200	7.52	1.62	1.62	.12
6. Business Managers	50	3.74	NA	NA	NA
7. College Students	60	1.88	NA	NA	NA

produced by insecurity? Can achievement activity be compensatory in nature?

The Affiliation Need as Insecurity: Other Investigations

Abraham Maslow has noted that all people experience the need to be liked. But an individual whose need to be liked runs rampant over all other personality needs is a person who is dependent on others. In Maslow's terms, such a person is unlikely to be "self-actualized." Maslow (1973:243) relates:

> (The person with a strong need for safety, belongingness and love relations) ... *must* be to an extent "other-directed" and *must* be sensitive to other people's approval, affection and good will. This is the same as saying that he must adopt and adjust by being flexible and responsive and by changing himself to fit the external situation. *He* is the dependent variable; the environment is the fixed, independent variable (Maslow's italics).

In a similar vein, Shiply and Veroff (1952) have maintained that the need for affiliation arises from a need for security, and Atkinson and his colleagues (1954) have viewed the affiliation motive as associated with a strong concern for social acceptance. Other research (for example, Boyatzis, 1973) has tended to support the notion that affiliation motivation as measured through thematic apperception identifies fear of rejection.

McClelland and his associates have found that the need for affiliation is associated with a behavioral syndrome that represents the need for approval. This syndrome includes a tendency for conformance (to group pressure), a preference for cooperative rather than competitive work climates, a lack of concern for task accomplishment unless it is instrumental in building interpersonal relations, a strong concern for how others view the self, and cautious goal setting in risk-taking situations.

Administrative Man and His Need to Affiliate

The administrative man experiences a twofold sense of insecurity. The first element of insecurity concerns his strong belief in personal causation and the attendant sense of personal responsibility which that belief implies. This type of leader reflects, "I alone am responsible for my future, my success and failure. Can I make it?" The second element of insecurity is an outgrowth of the first. Here the administrative man asks himself, "How do I look to other people? . . . Do they think I can make it?" The administrative man experiences anxiety not only when he evaluates himself and his organizational stature but also when he thinks about the ways in which others evaluate him. Administrative man is concerned with gaining respect—self-respect and the respect of others (see Table 5.8).

His struggle is clearly not (as is the case with the existential type of leader) a struggle for power with powerful others. His struggle is fought within himself. It is primarily a struggle for self-acceptance.

The lack of self-esteem and his experience of anxiety when being evaluated by others would lead us to hypothesize that this type of leader constantly concerns himself with the need to be liked. Expressions of a strong need to affiliate would provide us with some convergent evidence in support of this hypothesis. Analysis of stories written in response to our TATs suggest that this is indeed the case. The administrative man displays more affiliation motivation than either the rational or existential men or the military and business populations as a whole. Though mean differences fail to meet conventional levels of statistical significance, we do have convergent evidence for this assertion. Our administrative men also score considerably higher than either of the matched samples of business managers or college students who did not participate in this study.[7]

The concern that the administrative man displays for others comes out not only when we examine the stories he writes in response to TATs but also when we examine his feelings about his achievements. One "administrative" colonel was asked, "Please describe your feelings and thoughts after attaining a long sought-after goal." His response: "I am happy and ready to *share* with those who contributed" (italics supplied). This concern that others be recognized for their contributions is alien to many kinds of leaders. The existential man is such a leader. He displays concern only for

Table 5.8: "When you are required to direct the activities of others, how often do you receive their personal respect?" (%)

Group	N	Always/ Very Often	Often	Sometimes/ Rarely
1. Administrative Man	23	30.4	56.5	13.0
2. Rational Man	41	79.1	16.3	0.0
3. Existential Man	22	77.3	22.7	0.0
4. Whole Business Elite	50	67.4	28.2	4.2
5. Whole Military Elite	192	53.2	37.2	7.3

$X^2 = 22.96$, p. $< .001$ (Groups 1, 2, and 3).
$X^2 = 9.28$, p. $< .07$ (Groups 1, 4, and 5).

his reputation and fears public recognition of others. It would surely be anathema for him actually to encourage the recognition of others, for he must create impact.

The strong need for achievement expressed by the administrative man arises not out of a sense of self-esteem or the need to create impact through innovative activity. The need for achievement is strongly bound up with affiliation needs, or this leader's strong desire to be positively evaluated or held in esteem by others.[8] The achievement motive, then, is here not an expression of intrinsic motivation nor does it appear to derive from a sense of personal efficacy or self-confidence. It is an outgrowth of the need to be liked.

Similarly, this leader's sense of trust is not bound up with his experience of control. If this were so, it would suggest that the administrative man trusts others because he is sure of the nature and content of their actions (that is, he trusts them because he can count on them and they are not threatening). Correlation analysis reveals that the administrative man trusts his colleagues primarily because he fears they may reject him.[9]

The administrative man, then, has little reason to mistrust his fellow workers because his anxiety is centered around his own capabilities rather than the imposing capabilities of others. He imagines that expressions of hostility, mistrust, or even impoliteness would undermine fulfillment of his strong need for approval. He therefore appeals to group sentiments and expresses a desire to belong (Whyte, 1956).

Our evidence suggests that this leader's excessive concern with achievement-related activity is associated with a twofold sense of insecurity. These feelings of insecurity arise both because the administrative man is fearful of the way he is being evaluated by his colleagues and because he sees himself as solely responsible for his actions. Bereft of responsibility, devoid of the knowledge that man acts alone, there can be no anxiety. The man who absolves himself of his destiny is a man who can blame others for his failures.

Achieving behavior leads to eventual mobility within the organization and a set of rewards commensurate with the achievements of a mobile and successful man. Achievement brings status, and status provides administrative man with the symbols of success. These symbols of success bolster his looking-glass experience of self-worth.[10]

Because he is fearful of the way in which he is viewed by others, we would predict that the administrative man relates to people in a cautious, concerned fashion. His tendency to become entangled in the emotions of others allows us to predict further that he relates to his colleagues in a manner almost diametrically opposed to the powerful, dispassionate style that characterizes the existential man. Evidence presented in Table 5.9 indicates that this is so. The administrative man is less extroverted and less

Table 5.9: Administrative Man: His Sense of Dominance, Extroversion, and Persuasiveness*

Group	Dominance			Extroversion			Persuasiveness		
	X	t	p value	X	t	p value	X	t	p value
1. Administrative Man (N = 23)	2.74 (SD = 1.01)			1.87 (SD = 0.81)			3.30 (SD = 0.92)		
2. Rational Man (N = 43)	3.14 (SD = 1.06)	−1.51	.14	2.74 (SD = 1.00)	−3.83	.001	3.23 (SD = 1.27)	−0.26	NS
3. Existential Man (N = 22)	3.41 (SD = 1.14)	−2.08	.04	2.50 (SD = 0.80)	−2.62	.01	3.50 (SD = 1.30)	0.58	NS
4. Whole Military Elite (N = 56)	3.00 (SD = 1.23)	1.00	NS	2.47 (SD = 0.84)	2.95	.005	3.00 (SD = 1.15)	1.26	NS
5. Whole Military Elite (N = 244)	3.06 (SD = 1.06)	0.92	NS	2.48 (SD = 0.91)	3.35	.002	2.84 (SD = 1.14)	2.23	.03

*For all three personality characteristics the range is 1 to 5, with a score of 5 indicating a maximum score.

domineering than his peers. He is also less "persuasive" than either the rational or existential leader type (though he is more persuasive than many leaders in the whole military population).

This evidence is quite consistent with the imagery he expresses via thematic apperception. Here, the administrative man shows he is not concerned with maintaining influence over others, nor does he seek to create impact.When he does express visions of power, the administrative man does so not out of fear but purely out of hope (the Pearson correlation between his need for power and hope for power is .93, p $<$.001).[11] His anxiety does not emanate from a fear of powerful others or the need to bring an incomprehensible world under reign. His need system seeks the approval of others and not control of them. Coding for incidents of verbal hostility, use of force, influence attempts, and concern with hierarchic relations, a content analysis of all TAT protocols has shown that the administrative man is only marginally power-oriented. While existential leaders write stories that involve incidents of power-related themes over 36 percent of the time, administrative man expresses such themes at a rate of only 15 percent.

The anxiety that administrative men experience is not caused by a clash with exogenous forces that intervene and act against the attainment of personal goals. It derives from a struggle we all face, but one that figures most prominently in the life of the leader who strives for approval—" How much, and how often, must I compromise myself so that I may be accepted by others? How closely allied should my personal and professional goals be, and how closely allied are they? Must I conform to get ahead?"

THE ADMINISTRATIVE MAN AS SELF-STARTER

The traditional and rather uncomplimentary view of bureaucratic man is that of a conformer. His duties are routinized, his dress homogenized. His efforts are duplicated by dozens of others so they must be unoriginal. His prefabricated home reflects his blandness and lack of originality. His conspicuous consumption is interrupted only by his struggle with crab-grass. He is a pitiful creature if ever there was one, a faceless "cog in the machine." His strategy to get ahead involves conformity:

> These are the men who keep alert, look smart, avoid missteps, and attempt to show up well on assignments or in group policy discussion. They have ideas if requested and otherwise find cogent reasons for supporting the wisdom of the boss' ideas. They learn golf, join the right clubs, think the right thoughts. Their wives are attractive, but not brazen, entertain the right people, and suggest that John is brilliant as well as

> hard-working, a dedicated corporate servant, but also a wonderful
> husband and father. (Moore, 1969: 386)

However true this stereotypical characterization may be, the traditional view suffers from oversimplification and a general lack of understanding and empathy. There are, of course, bureaucratic leaders who are
only efficient at obeying the instructions of superiors. And it is surely true
that many "organization men" play strictly by the rules of the game,
forever emphasizing company policy and precedent. But the "bureaucratic
virtuoso" as Merton (1968) has called this type of leader, is a real person
struggling with the same problem we all face: How do we resolve the
discrepancy between our private goals and desires and our professional
aspirations?

In the case of the powerful leader, the struggle becomes greatly
intensified. The powerful leader commands great responsibility for people
and scarce resources. His decisions affect not only himself and his family
but hundreds, even thousands, of others. The powerful leader is a symbol,
both to himself and to the people who surround him. His office stands for
something greater than the man. People expect more because he is the
company president or the commanding officer. He expects more and
demands more of himself because he is the president or the chief executive
officer ("I am the president, I must therefore act like one"). The leader is
aware of his symbolic stature and aware of the increased demands placed
upon him both by himself and others.

In trying to resolve the natural contradiction between private needs
and professional aspirations, many powerful leaders feel compelled to
accept organizational norms. The combination of rewards received for
system maintenance and the risks to be taken for disrupting a system
governed by habituation makes it very difficult for bureaucratic leaders to
be great innovators. It is only the exceptional leader who is willing to risk
his stature and stability for innovative change. The administrative man is
not such a leader. He specializes in system maintenance, though on
occasion he may buck the system. For this type of leader, the risk
associated with initiative taking is greater than the reward. This young and
powerful leader has risen to the pinnacle of his profession, yet he does not
seek to alter his organization or its basic values. Why should he? The
values of his organization make him what he is.

The existential leader only in part derives his identity from the
organization. As he is controlled by outside forces his failures are blamed
on outside agents. In times of dismay, he believes it is the organization that
has failed him, and not he the organization. The intensification of the
struggle with personal goals and professional aspirations is most striking
with the administrative man. This leader is not controlled by outside

forces. Should he fail it will be due to his own inadequacies and not the whim of chance.

CONFORMANCE AND WORLD VIEW

In Chapter 1 it was stated that there is some self-starter and some organization man in all bureaucratic elites. Self-starter and organization man are ideal characterizations. In flesh and blood, they are not pure forms. All leaders must take initiatives at some time or another, and this is one important way in which they get ahead. But the variegated ways in which they do take initiatives, and the reasons why they take initiatives, differ greatly from leadership type to leadership type. The assumption of this work has been that leaders act in ways that are congruent with their view of the world and their experience of reality. Leadership styles represent a way of coping with the bureaucratic world as dictated by differing internal states of mind. As Barber has written in the introduction to *Presidential Character* (1972: vi):

> "Man copes. To each situation he brings resources from his past, organized in patterns which have helped him cope before. He copes with a situation not only as a structure of realities, but also as a *construction of his perception* (of that reality) (italics added)."

The rational man lives in a stable and ordered world. He can maximize his chances of success through rational problem solving, instrumental coalition building, and general attempts at deciphering the nature of a comprehensible reality. Existential man dwells in an irrational and absurd world governed by uncontrollable and incomprehensible forces. His intentions and his outcomes seem not to be related, thus his actions are not wholly "rational" in the classic sense of the word. Reason is not enough—the existential leader is immured by the need to control the chaotic world in which he dwells.

Not unlike the rational man, the administrative man experiences a comprehensible and ordered world. It all makes sense. Yet this leader is not certain whether he has the capacity, the where-with-all, to succeed. His leadership style reflects the ways in which he copes with his version of an uncertain self in a certain world.

Initiative taking is a vehicle by which leaders satisfy personal needs. Rational man takes initiatives in order to satisfy his need to solve and understand the problems of his world. Existential man takes initiatives in order to exercise his need for control. The initiative taking of administrative man is compensatory in nature. He takes initiatives in order to validate his sense of self-worth and to improve his uncertain image as viewed through the eyes of others.

THE NEED ACHIEVER IN BUREAUCRATIC STRUCTURES

At this juncture it is necessary to discuss an apparent contradiction that may have crossed the mind of our reader. The contradiction is this: The high need achiever has been characterized by McClelland and dozens of others as goal-directed and problem-solving-oriented. He will experiment with change, he will travel more than the individual with a low need to achieve, and he will try out new things. He has often been viewed as an innovator. The administrative man, marked by a prepotent need to achieve has been portrayed as a scion of the organization. (We have hesitated to call him a conformist for that would be inappropriate. He is however, an organizational loyalist.) Is it not contradictory to portray this need achiever as a "conformist" (if we may use the word now to emphasize a point)?

A simple, monocausal explanation might conclude that it is. But as we have tried to show, a person is not just a "need achiever," a "power seeker," "externally located," "confident," "trusting," or any single quality. He is all these and much, much more that we do not know, in varying degrees. Leadership style is a function of multiple causative factors. The administrative man is a very high need achiever, but he also expresses strong fears of rejection. "Administrative man" is an umbrella label used to convey an image of a class of leaders whose more or less shared personality characteristics are highly complex. The point is that as we examine the whole ensemble of personality relations, we could see that though he does express need achievement behavior, this behavior is tempered by other personality influences and especially the need to be liked by others.

The administrative man believes his goals are less his own than even the existential man, a type of leader whose fate is perceived as being determined by outside forces. Table 5.10 offers some striking evidence that in spite of his strong need to achieve, the administrative man selects goals that are consistent with the expectations of others. Still, it is important to point out that though he does base many of his goals on the expectations of others, almost 40 percent claim their goals are either "completely" or "very much" their own. This is something not many of us could honestly claim.

There is little reason to believe that the administrative man responds to the expectations of others in the way that the traditional literature suggests—as an automaton, unaware of his sense of personal compromise. It is our belief that the elite respondents in this study, a highly educated, intelligent, and perceptive group of people, are aware of the clash between

Table 5.10: "To what extent do you believe your life's goals are truly your own, and how much are the result of others' expectations?" (%)

Group	"My goals are..." Completely My Own	Very Much My Own	Largely My Own	Not So Much My Own
1. Administrative Man	4.3	34.8	56.5	4.3
2. Rational Man	27.9	58.1	9.3	4.6
3. Existential Man	31.8	36.4	31.8	0.0
4. Whole Business Elite	20.0	36.0	40.0	4.0
5. Whole Military Elite	18.6	35.1	40.7	5.2

$X^2 = 20.61$, p. $< .005$ (Groups 1, 2, and 3).
$X^2 = 4.10$, NS (Groups 1, 4, and 5).

101

personal goals and professional aspirations. These people are aware of the magnitude of their compromises. Frequent compromise is not without its attendant frustrations.

Duty: A Variant of Conformance?

As the administrative man has a great sense of responsibility, he is often apt to expend effort working on tasks that he finds neither meaningful nor enjoyable. But because of his organizational allegiance and because many uninteresting tasks must (as a role demand) be done, he does them.

The administrative man does not firmly believe that it is the duty of everyone to do the job the very best he can. But when we ask the administrative man how often his work has meaning and how often his work is just a duty, it's another story (see Tables 5.11 and 5.12). The data presented in Tables 5.11 and 5.12 are not dramatic. But taken together with what we know about this leader's psychological makeup, it is apparent that the impulse of personal responsibility is salient. Exactly 50 percent of the administrative men feel that "most of the time" or "sometimes" their work is just a duty (that is, it is not personally meaningful). We do not mean to equate duty with conformance, nor do we mean to imply that only the administrator values duty. Duty to one's organization can assume a multiplicity of forms, as one can loyally serve one's organization in various ways. Yet the cognitive characteristics of the administrative man, and in particular his need for social approval, provide this leader with a strong sense of duty.

We have seen that this type of leader selects goals that are consistent (if not congruent) with the expectations of others. He is also apt to engage in his work not because it has any special meaning but because to do otherwise would be irresponsible. Can we present any evidence that the administrative man believes in the inevitable necessity of conformance? Can the private need for personal responsibility and acceptance be publically dressed in the guise of organizational loyalty?

It appears that it can. The administrative man, unlike many of his colleagues, believes strongly that conformity is a terminal necessity, and not a phase to end. For this type of organizational leader, duty, a sense of loyalty, and, ultimately, conformism have interrelated meanings. First, they represent the transformation of the psychological need for personal responsibility into a socially accepted and organizationally valued form, and second, they represent a proven strategy to get ahead. For this type of leader, the institutionally sanctioned notion of duty becomes a reified mechanism by which private needs are satisfied. While the "conformist" is the object of social disapprobation, the dutiful "loyalist" is many a splendorous thing. For the administrative man, a type of leader who is

Table 5.11: "It is the duty of each person to do his job the very best he can" (%)

Groups	N	Strongly Agree	Agree	Slightly Agree/Disagree
1. Administrative Man	23	47.8	39.1	13.0
2. Rational Man	43	79.1	18.6	0.0
3. Existential Man	22	64.5	36.4	0.0
4. Whole Business Elite	50	58.0	36.0	6.0
5. Whole Military Elite	194	64.9	32.0	2.5

$X^2 = 10.23$, p. $< .03$ (Groups 1, 2, and 3).
$X^2 = 7.56$, p. $< .12$ (Groups 1, 4, and 5).

Table 5.12: "Americans today are preoccupied with finding meaning in their lives and in their jobs. How often do you find your work personally meaningful and how often just a duty?" (%)

Groups	N	"My work is just a duty . . . "		
		Most of the time/Sometimes	Not very often	Never
1. Administrative Man	19	50.0	36.4	0.0
2. Rational Man	39	14.1	58.1	18.6
3. Existential Man	41	35.2	47.0	17.6
4. Whole Business Elite	41	22.4	51.0	10.2
5. Whole Military Elite*	166	51.3	33.5	1.6

*This is one of the few instances in which the business and military populations differed dramatically. The direction of the data is consistant with what we would expect.

$X^2 = 12.84$, p. < .01 (Groups 1, 2, and 3).
$X^2 = 21.05$, p. < .001 (Groups 1, 4, and 5).

especially sensitive to the clash between private goals and personal expectations, "duty" (sometimes seen by his colleagues as conformance) is an anxiety-reducing mechanism (see Table 5.13).

INITIATIVE TAKING AND INTERPERSONAL RELATIONS

In our discussion of administrative man and his sense of trust, we noted that this type of leader was both generally trusting and especially trustful of superiors. This trust does not apparently encourage the administrative man to present superiors with unsolicited recommendations. Only 39 percent report doing so "always" or "very often." It is within the realm of possibility that this sense of trust (which is especially strong with regard to superiors) is really "courtly deference," an interpersonal strategy intended to flatter others as well as enhance the administrative man's own stature.

As a non-power-oriented, nondominant high need achiever, this type of leader does not direct his initiative-taking efforts toward powerful others. He has no compelling need to impress or outperform his colleagues, and his looking-glass sense of self only seems to inhibit the presentation of unsolicited recommendations. We have no evidence that the administrative man is for any reason unable to formulate such

Table 5.13: Administrative Man: His Feelings About Conformity

"It is a popular notion that in order to achieve success in an organization one must conform to the expectations of others. Is this conformity only necessary at lower levels, to end when higher positions are reached, or will conformity always be a necessity?" (%)

Groups	N	A phase to end, top management can be creative	Conformity is always a necessity
1. Administrative Man	17	13.6	63.6
2. Rational Man	29	34.9	32.6
3. Existential Man	17	41.5	55.6
4. Whole Business Elite	40	35.4	47.9
5. Whole Military Elite	135	22.8	47.2

$X^2 = 5.22$, p. $< .08$ (Groups 1, 2, and 3).
$X^2 = 3.43$, p. $< .17$ (Groups 1, 4, and 5).

recommendations, but he suffers from anxiety when bringing these recommendations to the attention of others. His fear of rejection and disapproval strongly attentuates initiative taking. His fear is not taking the initiative or making the recommendation, it is the fear of negative evaluation by others. When he does take initiative, he is highly uncertain that his recommendations will be acted upon (see Table 5.14). In initiative taking situations where the administrative man must directly influence or interact with others, he is uncertain and consequently less a self-starter than either the rational or existential leader (men characterized as dominant, extroverted, and power-oriented).[12]

The affiliative leadership style leads to strain in interpersonal relations. The administrative man fears that attempts at stimulating the ambitions of associates will be interpreted by his colleagues as attempts at personal gain. And to a large degree he is correct. Characterized by high (avoidance) affiliation, this leader seeks the approval of others; attempts to care for and help others as a way of making himself important to them; seeks to be with others who are perceived as being similar to himself in an attempt to build his sense of self-worth; and seeks to evaluate himself through comparison with others (Boyatzis, 1973:271).

Typical of the affiliative style is one corporate vice-president who said, "I have a strong need to succeed. And a very strong need to be accepted by people. I feel some insecurity and some self-doubt about how competent I am. I want to play the game if I can win and gain respect. . . . Winning is not really it—it's not the right thing to say. It's really the need for respect from my peers" (Maccoby, 1976:87).

Table 5.14: "When you do present superiors with unsolicited recommendations, usually how certain are you that these recommendations will be acted upon?" (%)

Groups	N	Usually Certain	Certain/ Somewhat Uncertain	Uncertain
1. Administrative Man	23	17.4	65.2	17.4
2. Rational Man	43	76.7	23.3	0.0
3. Existential Man	22	72.7	27.3	0.0
4. Whole Business Elite	50	54.0	42.0	4.0
5. Whole Military Elite	192	41.2	51.0	6.7

$X^2 = 28.85$, p. $< .001$ (Groups 1, 2, and 3).
$X^2 = 10.86$, p. $< .03$ (Groups 1, 4, and 5).

The administrative man is tentative and cautious when relating to others. His excessive concern with the approval of others deters him from assuming the bold, decisive, powerful, and detached posture maintained by other kinds of leaders, yet his looking-glass sense of self prevents him from being inflexible or unyielding in his decision-making role. As he is extrasensitive to other people's approval, he must be malleable and responsive to other's demands. He must master an anxiety-reducing and socially valued tool—that of compromise.

While the conflict arena provides the existential man with the opportunity to show his mettle and display his wares (power-dominant behaviors and strategies of style), the administrative man must (in order to satisfy his needs) practice conflict avoidance.[13] An independent measure of "activity-passivity" indicates that indeed administrative men are significantly less "active" than rational or existential men.[14]

As administrative man fears the disapproval of others, he eschews personal competition and especially its most extreme public form, interpersonal confrontation. The administrative man is a careerist. He wants no part of losing and at the same time he shies away from exacting loss from others. This would violate his need for their positive evaluation and regard and thus the enhancement of his weak self-image.

Process-Directed Initiative Taking

The initiative-taking style of administrative man is not people-directed but "process-directed." Where initiative taking must include motivating, persuading, stimulating, or enhancing others' performance, or esprit de corps, or in any way making others feel powerful or integral to the decision-making process, administrative man is deficient. Properly speaking, he is not a leader, but a manager. His excessive concern with the approval of others, coupled with his strong need for achievement, makes the management of people less psychologically satisfying than the management of ideas.

While there is substantial evidence that the classic need achiever directs his efforts toward energetic and creative challenge seeking, we have little direct evidence that the administrative man seeks challenges more frequently either publicly or in the private technical realm (that is, the realm of the problem-solving craftsman). What is apparent is that the frequency with which the administrative man seeks challenges is less than that of the other two leadership types. Only 26 percent of administrators actively seek challenges "always" or "very often," as compared with 72 percent of rational men, 82 percent of existential men, 64 percent of whole business elite, and 40 percent of the military (see Table 5.15).

The evidence presented in Table 5.15 is cumulative and consistent with our portrayal of this leadership type. Our data indicate that high need achievement alone does not result in the taking of challenges in the bureaucratic milieu.[15]

We do have evidence that this type of leader responds primarily to process challenges or challenges that crop up in the normal course of his daily workload. This may be contrasted with nonprocess challenges or challenges that must actively be created in spite of the routinization of the daily workload. We have stressed that it is the active pursuit of challenges that characterizes the real self-starter. How does the administrative man match up against the self-starter in the rational and existential elite?

It is apparent from Table 5.16 that the administrative man both actively creates challenges and becomes motivated by process challenges (or those that appear on his desk). But it is significant that almost half the administrative men primarily respond to challenges placed before them in the course of their daily work. This leader, like other leaders, takes initiatives in a style that is supportive of and congruent with his fundamental need system. He does what is expected of him, for such behavior is essential to the healthy functioning of his need for approval (which in turn is necessary for the enhancement of his looking-glass self). As he is dependent upon others for the satisfaction of his prepotent personality needs, he cannot risk the bold maneuver. Such action could lead to failure and social disapprobation.

SITUATIONAL AMBIGUITY

The bureaucratic leader who becomes intimidated under conditions of risk is not likely to feel comfortable making decisions in the absence of an organizational precedent. The administrative man appears to be such a leader. His cautious manner when relating to others, his reliance on socially accepted norms and cues, and his fear of disapproval make a detached, decisive posture difficult to maintain. We would therefore predict that this type of leader is especially apt to feel anxious when having to deal with situational ambiguity.

Surprisingly, however, the administrative man is not all that much more uncomfortable than many of his colleagues. He certainly shows less anxiety than we hypothesized. Over 85 percent feel only slight discomfort or no discomfort at all in making decisions about which there exist no organizational ground rules or precedents.

Table 5.15: "About how often do you go out and seek new challenges?" (%)

Group	N	Always	Very Often	Often	Not Very Often
1. Administrative Man	23	0.0	26.1	47.8	26.0
2. Rational Man	43	25.6	46.5	23.3	4.6
3. Existential Man	22	17.8	64.2	17.8	0.0
4. Whole Business Elite	50	8.0	56.0	32.0	4.0
5. Whole Military Elite	194	4.1	36.1	41.2	18.6

$X^2 = 23.79$, p. $< .001$ (Groups 1, 2, and 3).
$X^2 = 15.32$, p. $< .02$ (Groups 1, 4, and 5).

109

Table 5.16: "Would you consider yourself a person who actively looks for challenges or someone who becomes motivated primarily through challenges that appear on your desk?" (%)

Groups	N	I actively look for challenges	I become motivated by challenges that appear on my desk
1. Administrative Man	23	52.2	47.8
2. Rational Man	42	86.0	9.3
3. Existential Man	22	90.9	9.0
4. Whole Business Elite	50	78.0	20.0
5. Whole Military Elite	193	70.1	27.8

$X^2 = 14.10$, $p < .001$ (Groups 1, 2, and 3).
$X^2 = 5.04$, $p. < .08$ (Groups 1, 4, and 5).

THE SELF-STARTER NEEDS LITTLE ENCOURAGEMENT

Just as we hypothesized that administrative men would be uncomfortable in new work situations, we also hypothesized that they would have a strong need for encouragement. Unlike our previous hypothesis, however, this one seems to be confirmed.

Nearly 22 percent of administrators reported that they needed encouragement "always" or "very often." This may be contrasted with only 2 percent of rational men and 4 percent of existential men. On the other hand, almost one-third of the administrative group reported that they "rarely" or "never" needed encouragement. This suggests that there is some self-starter in the administrative man. Our evidence, however, suggests that this manager takes personal initiatives most often in problem-solving realms (where he is confident of his technical abilities) rather than in the interpersonal realm (where he experiences a fear of disapproval by others).

It is becoming evident that the administrative man is not as reliant as perhaps he is often made out to be. As a craftsman or technician, this careerist needs relatively little encouragement. When encouragement is needed, this manager seeks it most frequently from superiors and least frequently from friends and loved ones outside the organization. Compared with other leadership types, the administrative man is also very peer-oriented.[16]

For each administrator who reported needing encouragement from friends and loved ones, two reported needing encouragement from superiors (people inside the organization). This runs counter to the social support needs reported by the other leaders in this study and illustrates that the administrative man needs professional nurturance. This idiosyncratic pattern of need for encouragement is a reflection of professional insecurity. It is essential that the administrative man be reminded of his importance through the continued attention and mutual respect of the people with whom he works. The interactive and affective process that provides interpersonal encouragement is one (of many) mechanisms by which this need may be satisfied and his insecurity buoyed. To receive encouragement indicates that one is important to the continued functioning of the group. To be encouraged is to be part of the group. Ultimately it represents the granting of approval by valued others.

GOAL ATTAINMENT

Immediately upon completion of an arduous task or the successful attainment of a long sought-after goal, the self-starter reaches out for new, as yet unresolved challenges. His general sense of uneasiness prevents him from resting. He ceaselessly acts to take on more and more. It is not the successful completion of the task that gratifies him but the successful meeting of the challenge. Satisfaction comes from sheer accomplishment rather than from the glory of the accomplished goal. The self-starter has no defined point at which to stop, though he always has a place to go. In his study of over 100 business executives, W. E. Henry (1949) reported that the "need to keep moving" was one of the group's most important shared features. Unfortunately, wrote Henry, the constant motivation of his executives could not be shut off.

We have mixed evidence for the assertion that the administrative man ceaselessly pursues challenges, never stopping to "shut off" his general sense of activation. In an attempt to examine how motivated leaders feel directly following goal attainment, all respondents were asked to "describe their thoughts and feelings upon completion of a long sought-after goal." The administrative man responds to the question in a manner that is consistent with our model of the self-starter. Some examples of responses written by administrative men follow:

> I am fulfilled, satisfied with the accomplishment, but consider the next goal.

> I am emotionally drained, I feel a sense of withdrawal, and (I am) unable to focus on detail.

> I have even more confidence in my abilities and gain inertia.

> I feel relief and I am happy with myself.

> I enjoy it for a period of time and face up to the next task.

> I feel extensive relief of pressure.

> I am happy that I endured to the conclusion, (was) persistent and didn't give up.

> I feel relief and have an urge to begin something new.

> I question whether the success was worth the effort, and whether I can exploit the success to gain further goals.

> I am relieved that the long struggle has ended, then go on and seek another goal.

A number of themes emerge. Perhaps the two most prominent are relief of some kind of unspecified pressure and the sense of having to "face up to" or otherwise pursue new goals (over 21 percent of this leadership type mentioned the need for seeking new goals as part of their response to this question). The experience of having released some reservoir of energy in pursuit of the goal is comon. The belief that this signifies only temporary satisfaction is also common. Goal attainment apparently does not have an enduring effect on the administrative man's level of activation, or as one colonel said, his "urge" to begin anew.

The most important aspect of this type of leader's feelings upon goal accomplishment is his experience of relief. To be relieved implies freeing oneself of something uncomfortable—to lessen or alleviate, to rid oneself or release oneself from something that produces stress, disquietude or anxiety. The self-starter builds up, or somehow sustains, an intense level of anxiety while pursuing his goals. Upon goal completion, he experiences ephemeral relief, momentarily freeing himself from his discomfort. Yet he always maintains an urge to accomplish more, to build up his reservoir of pressure, his constructive impulse once again, only to find short-lived solace upon its release. And the next goal has its attendant anxieties. And so on. Only goal accomplishment brings relief.

Taken together with what we know about the administrative man's personal need system, this is convincing evidence that anxiety is related to (though not necessarily a sufficient cause of) initiative taking.

Despite his continuous urge to accomplish new goals, the administrative man feels less compelled than his colleagues to seek new professional plateaus. Over one-quarter (the highest percentage of all leadership types) report that they are content with their present position and would remain so if for some reason they could not be promoted to a higher level. In addition, about 30 percent claim they have already reached the professional plateau they had set for themselves upon entering professional life. This feeling of professional contentedness runs counter to our general theory that the self-starter is never content—either with his short-range technical successes or with his professional accomplishments. He must always search for something "higher" than his present condition.

OVERVIEW OF THE ADMINISTRATIVE MAN

What has emerged in this chapter is a consistent picture of the administrative man as an insecure but technically competent and energetic careerist hampered by a weakened (looking glass) self-image. His very strong need for achievement provides him with an energetic motive disposition that he directs toward problem solving and initiative taking in "process" realms. Yet his prepotent need for approval attenuates initiative taking in the interpersonal domain. What we have shown is the merging of personality and leadership style. The character of this type of manager is directly and systematically related to his perception of the world and the way he behaves in that world. Table 5.17 brings together some of the diverse themes we have discussed and illustrates the intimate relationship between personality, world view, and style.

The individual uses the organization to satisfy his needs while simultaneously the organization uses the individual to satisfy its demands. This conflicted yet symbiotic relationship represents the reconciliation of discordant personal and organizational goals. The successful and growth-oriented organization cannot afford to satisfy its needs only. To do so would be to neglect the self-actualization of its member parts.

CONCLUSION: THE ADMINISTRATIVE MAN AND THE THEORY OF THE SELF-STARTER

The self-starter is a hybrid of Lasswell's political man. The theory of the self-starter predicts that organizational challenge seeking and other forms of professional initiative taking are the result of personal drives that seek the satisfaction of private needs. If this were entirely true, then the twofold sense of insecurity experienced by administrative man would somehow propel him to self-starterdom.

We do have evidence that this leader responds well to challenges that crop up in the normal course of his daily affairs. Yet it does seem reasonable to conclude that the administrative man's experience of anxiety is perhaps more debilitating than constructive. His weak self-image and his strong need for approval prevent this type of man from being either a bold leader of men or a cool risk taker. Neither a "leader" nor an "entrepreneur,"

Table 5.17: Administrative Man: His Character and Behavior

Character	Behavior
Internal Experience of Control	Strong Sense of Responsibility
Insecurity	Dislike of Competition
Not Domineering; Introverted	Process Rather Than People-Directed
Very Strong Affiliation Needs	Approval-Seeking
Very Strong Need for Achievement	Problem-Solving Mindedness, Technical Competence
Strong Feelings of Anxiety	Cautious Risk-Taking
Trusting	Deferential

this "manager" expresses himself through process-oriented tasks and receives satisfaction only through the explicit (rather than tacit) approval granted by others. His dependence upon other people both for satisfaction and positive self-regard makes him generally incapable of assuming positions that require a strong, commanding posture or an innovative style.

There is no simple relationship between insecurity and activism. There are at least two reasons for this: There is a point at which insecurity reaches an effective threshold—at that point, insecurity transposes itself into debilitating anxiety; and insecurity is of many types, appears in varying degrees (and under varying circumstances), and encourages "reaction-formations" of many forms.

NOTES

1. The conflict between personal goals and professional expectations is a central theme in the work of Chris Argyris. In at least two of his books (*Interpersonal Competence and Organizational Effectiveness*, 1969; *Personality and Organization*, 1959), this theme receives a place of prominence. From the view of the organization, it is essential to try and bring personal and organizational goals together. This makes work more satisfying for the manager while increasing productivity.

2. The process of the individual "using" the organization to fulfill his needs and simultaneously the organization "using" the individual to achieve its demands has been called the "fusion process" (Bakke, 1955).

3. Among the group of administrative men we find three directors of multinational corporations, two vice-presidents, three colonels, and two majors who have been promoted in an accelerated fashion.

4. A more than tacit assumption of the locus of control literature is just this—people who are internally located are thought to be personally efficacious. Yet the published evidence for this assertion is rather sketchy, and our own data on existential man seem to indicate that the presumed link is rather tenuous. For an examination of the assumed link between internal perceptions of control and achievement in large organizations, the reader is referred to Rothberg (1980).

5. A glance at locus of control scores for "normal" populations reveals that the administrative man is relatively internal. The population norms hover around 8.0 (Rotter, 1966; Harvey, 1971; Maroldo and Flachmeier, 1978), much the same as that of our whole business and military populations.

6. It is interesting to note that the administrative man, presumably encouraged as a child to master some form of activity, has not only a very strong need to achieve but he also displays a very strong sense of control The nurturance of these perceptions may originate in common upbringing experiences. For both the business and military elite groups tested, internal perceptions of control and need achievement have a Pearson correlation of .15, $p < .01$.

7. See Table 3.4 and its discussion for a description of the matched samples.

8. For administrative men, the need for affiliation and the need for achievement have an r of .62, $p < .02$.

9. Administrative man trusts his colleagues slightly more than most of the other leadership types. Mean differences in trust for administrative men and the whole business population are not statistically significant, though mean differences between administrators

and the whole military are (t = 2.67, p < .03). Among administrative men, fear of power and trust have a Pearson correlation of .60, p <.01. This is quite an important finding and provides some convergent evidence for our portrait of the administrative man as a leader whose struggle centers around the way in which he relates to other people.

10. Just how very important these symbols of success are cannot be exaggerated. Presthus (1962:183) remarks, "In business, status acquisition and reinforcement have become the subject of rational calculation. Standard Oil of California, for example, classifies executives from type 1, who merit drapes, wall-to-wall carpeting, private offices, walnut desks, etc., to type 4, with no private office or oak desks. . . . Some executives, it seems, have developed to a fine art the skill of being the first to acquire new status indexes, thus acquiring for themselves a sense of distinction."

11. The cited Pearson correlation between need for power and hope for power is somewhat overstated because fear of power (as a measurable construct) derives from the overall presence of need for power. By definition the two are, to a certain degree, associated. The magnitude of the association, however, is still exceedingly high.

12. The administrative man's high level of need achievement here does not come into play. Nor does it with the elite group as a whole. For all participants within the study, the Pearson correlation for stimulating the ambitions of associates and need achievement is −.10, p < .05.

13. In technical terms, the power motive that characterizes the existential leader is an approach disposition. The affiliation motive that characterizes the administrative man is one of avoidance.

14. When mean scores for administrative men are compared with mean scores for rational men, t = −2.89, p < .006; for administrative and existential men, t = −1.46, p < .15. Barber (1972) views the "active-passive" dimension as the single most important determinant of leadership style.

15. For the entire sample there is in fact a negative relationship between need achievement and the taking of initiatives (r = −.09, p < .05).

16. Forty-eight percent of administrative men indicated that they preferred encouragement from superiors (as opposed to their peers or loved ones outside the organization).

CHAPTER **6**

ENTREPRENEURIAL MAN

Since Max Weber's *Protestant Ethic and the Spirit of Capitalism* (1958) literally hundreds of investigators have sought to understand the effects of the Protestant ethos on the rise and growth of capitalism and its organizational forms. Eisenstadt (1968: 3) has said that "Weber's famous Protestant Ethic thesis, which attributed the rise of modern, as distinct from premodern types of capitalism to the influence of Protestantism ... has provided, probably more than any other single *specific thesis* in the social sciences, a continuous focus of scientific controversy."

At least two lines of analysis have emerged. The first, which is sociological in nature, concerns itself with that aspect of the Weber thesis which centers on the contribution of modern forms of religion (especially Protestantism) to the transformation of feudalism into capitalism. Thus Troeltsch (1912), Tawney (1926), and Eisenstadt (1968) have in one way or another tried to show how the entrepreneurial spirit of capitalism has accounted for the growth and development of capitalist (as opposed to premodern) nation-states.

The second line of analysis, which is more psychological in nature, has attempted to show how the ethos of religious asceticism has contributed to the rise of a historically unique entrepreneurial "class" (Lewis, 1955; Schumpeter, 1934; McClelland, 1961). Entrepreneurial men, it is presumed, imbued with the ethos of Protestantism, have in some unique way contributed to the rise of modern corporate organizations and their attendant forms of impersonality and rationalism (that is, division of labor, advanced bookkeeping, and so on).

This chapter offers an empirical test of that aspect of the Weber thesis which purports to show how Protestant asceticism has contributed to an acquisitive ethos, and in this, the underlying psychological drive in corporate man.

WEBER'S ENTREPRENEUR

Max Weber's famous work *The Protestant Ethic* portrayed the modern entrepreneur as driven by deeply rooted anxiety and doubt. This doubt arose because Weber's man was uncertain of his "other-worldly" destiny. Efforts to mitigate the anxiety that flowed from such doubt were, Weber believed, the most powerful force in the rise of the spirit of capitalism.

As his namesake implies, the entrepreneur is one who organizes, manages, and takes the risks associated with running an enterprise.[1] Yet he is plagued by doubt. He is anxious because his life is a test, the outcome of which determines his ultimate fate for all eternity—his place in heaven or hell. The psychological burden on Weber's entrepreneur was that of proving his self-worth.

In an attempt to make himself worthy of salvation (thereby eradicating his deeply rooted sense of doubt), the entrepreneur is driven to pursue ascetism in his private life and (the methodical and rational) accumulation of wealth in his public life. Ascetism, or self-denial, is a way of demonstrating how he is capable of resisting temptation, the first and most pernicious of obstacles blocking the path to salvation.[2] The rational accumulation of wealth is a way of demonstrating that he had fulfilled his obligation in the world. The pursuit of wealth

> as a fruit of labor in a calling was a sign of God's blessing, And even more important: the religious valuation of restless, continuous, systematic work in a worldly calling, (was) ... the highest means to ascetism, and at the same time the surest and most evident proof of rebirth and genuine faith, (and) must have been the most powerful conceivable lever for the expansion of that attitude toward life which we have here called the spirit of capitalism. (Weber, 1958: 172)

As the examplar of capitalist culture, entrepreneurial man is fascinating not only because he represents the personification of the capitalist ethic but also because he is a blend of some of the most intriguing paradoxes.

Among some of the more interesting relations of Weber's entrepreneur are these: (1) He cannot in any *rational* way acknowledge the existence of God—through an act of faith he believes in Him, and His capacity to somehow "select" those worthy of salvation; yet at the same time the entrepreneur's behavior is guided by rational calculation. (2) The entrepreneur is personally insecure and plagued with doubt, yet he labors with certainty. And (3), most importantly, his basically irrational fears embedded in faith promote the systematic and essentially rational pursuit of wealth. Thus, it was the entrepreneur's faith and not his reason that led to the methodical and systematic (that is, scientific) organization of labor. In short, the paragon of modern culture is an anxiety-driven mystic, and capitalism, embodying the most rational elements of organization, is the product of irrational man.

A reading of Weber's book reveals that Weber's entrepreneur was distinguished by three important personality characteristics. First, he believed that he lacked complete control of his fate. It was God and not he who determined his destiny. Second, the experience of being ultimately judged and controlled by a powerful, extrinsic force (God) fostered personal insecurity and doubt. Third, this insecurity in turn fostered a sense of personal repression or inhibition. The entrepreneur was plagued by anxiety for he was never certain of his fate. The absence of fate control, coupled with personal insecurity, produced an unfulfilled and anxiety-driven man whose purpose in life was to demonstrate his worth before God.

The presumed effects of entrepreneurial man's unique personality and his anxiety-ridden vision of the world were threefold: self-discipline or asceticism (attempts at proving self-worth through self-denial); an active orientation toward the world (attempts at proving self-worth through fulfillment of worldly obligations); and the rational pursuit of wealth (attempts at procuring the symbolic "currency" of God's acceptance by the most effective, efficient, and quickest way possible). Self-denial, worldly activity through a "calling," and the accumulation of wealth were thus intended to demonstrate the entrepreneur's worth before God (and himself) and release the entrepreneur from his agonizing sense of doubt.

The plausibility of the Protestant ethic thesis (and at the same time a source of its confusion) arises from Weber's implicit use of a powerful explanatory device—that of "reification." Weber maintained that the world view and ethos of the entrepreneurial class had, in its first instance, a religious foundation, and that this foundation was Protestant in nature.[3] But Weber believed that somehow this ethos had become reified, that is, a material part of daily life, and secularized. The secularization of initially religious sentiments and fears created new roles that allowed man to legitimately accumulate wealth. The imperative of the "calling," which was initially inculcated into Protestant peoples over time lost its divine implication and had acquired its own dynamic. Weber (1958: 53) believed that now the calling

is thought of so purely as an end in itself, that from the point of view of the happiness of, or utility to, the single individual, it appears entirely transcendental and absolutely irrational. Man is dominated by the making of money, by acquisition as the ultimate purpose of his life.

And, as Tawney (Weber, 1958: 3) has remarked, (for Weber) "labor is not merely an economic means, it is a spiritual end."

This is the key to understanding Weber's theory: Weber did not maintain that each entrepreneur consciously feared the might of God and His ability to "select" those worthy of salvation. He did believe that the secularization of initially religious imperatives created the historical and psychological precondition (or spirit) of the modern capitalist ethos.

TESTING WEBER'S THEORY

As dictated by our initial leadership typology (see Chapter 2) we isolated those leaders who both believe they lack control of their fate and are personally insecure. We must now see if, as predicted by the Weber theory, this leadership type experiences a great sense of inhibition; ascertain whether the absence of fate control is indeed the cause of the entrepreneur's insecurity (as Weber theorized), or whether (like other types of leaders) he is insecure for other reasons; and finally we must see if the unique personality cluster that we have called "enterpreneurial" is indeed the psychological substructure for an activistic ethos as Weber believed. Put most simply, we wish to investigate whether the unique constellation of "A" personality attributes causes "B" behaviors:

"A"	"B"
Lack of fate control	Self-discipline
Personal insecurity	Acquisitiveness
Inhibition	Activity orientation

In the first part of this chapter we will test the Weber thesis by examining the internal dynamics of the entrepreneurial man (or the interrelations of "A"). Here we wish to see if, as Weber theorized, the entrepreneur's lack of self-esteem derives from his experience of external control, and whether his insecurity fosters inhibition. In the second part we will investigate whether "A" causes "B" (that is, whether the entrepreneurial man is indeed an acquisitive activist).

Let us now turn to the entrepreneur and see if he behaves according to Weber's theory.

OUR ENTREPRENEUR: HIS WORLD VIEW

By definition, our entrepreneurial man, like that of Weber, believes his fate is exogenously determined. Over 75 percent agree with the statement,

"I often have little influence over the things that happen to me." Over 30 percent agree with the telling statement, "Leaders are born and not made." One entrepreneurial leader was asked, "Describe your feelings upon completion of a long sought-after goal." His response vividly illustrates how important the extrinsic sense of control figures in his life: "I feel a sense of relief that I have been able to achieve the goal without unforeseen circumstances having prevented it."

Not only does the entrepreneur experience little mastery over his personal fate, but likewise he feels powerless in influencing less proximate social affairs (see Table 6.1). Our entrepreneur, like Weber's, feels that his life is somehow influenced by forces that are beyond his control. Personal capabilities and intentions seem not to be consistently related to his desired outcomes.

Unlike other kinds of leaders such as Whyte's (1965) famous "organization man", the entrepreneur does not derive his identity from the organization. He is adrift, distantiated. Like Weber's entrepreneur who pursued innovation and wealth through work in small businesses and independent crafts, our entrepreneur eschews the organization and the structure which it imposes.[4] Table 6.2 shows that the entrepreneur mistrusts others and experiences a general sense of discomfort with his "place" in the organization. The world of entrepreneurial man is not benevolent, but threatening. His life is a trial.

Compared with either the business or military elite as a whole, the entrepreneur perceives himself to be both under the control of outside forces and insecure (see Table 6.3). It is important, however, for us to determine whether this insecurity derives from this leader's experience of being controlled by outside forces or whether it has its basis in other

Table 6.1: "As far as world affairs are concerned, most of us are the victims of forces we can neither control nor understand" (%)

Group	N	Agree	Disagree
1. Entrepreneurial Man	42	62.2	37.8
2. Rational Man	41	0.0	100.0
3. Existential Man	22	45.5	54.5
4. Administrative Man	23	8.7	91.3
5. Whole Business Elite	61	37.7	62.3
6. Whole Military Elite	226	22.5	75.2

$X^2 = 45.67$, p. $< .001$ (Groups 1 through 4).
$X^2 = 26.58$, p. $< .001$ (Groups 1, 5, and 6).

Table 6.2: The Entrepreneur and His Sense of Trust

Group	N	$\bar{X}$	SD	t	p value
1. Entrepreneurial Man	45	59.76	8.74		
2. Rational Man	42	67.60	10.14	3.85	.001
3. Existential Man	21	63.01	8.60	1.42	.16
4. Administrative Man	23	67.07	7.18	3.68	.001
5. Whole Business Elite	55	69.81	12.37	2.76	.007
6. Whole Military Elite	223	63.67	9.31	2.71	.009

infirmities of the self-image. Does the entrepreneur, as Weber would predict, become insecure as a result of his experience of being controlled by outside forces?

THE SOURCE OF THE ENTREPRENEUR'S INSECURITY

The insecurity of entrepreneurial man is not, as Weber hypothesized, primarily related to his experience of being controlled by outside forces. The Pearson correlation of external control and personal insecurity is only .09 (NS). More important is the fact that his insecurity is related to, or bound up with, other weaknesses of the self-image. For example, when asked to estimate his own IQ, the entrepreneur ranks it lower than do business and military groups treated either separately or as a whole.[5] Or, when asked the role that self-confidence has played in the attainment of his organizational success, he answers, "Very little." And less than the whole business and military groups as a whole does the entrepreneur report having the "will to lead." Moreover, 31 percent of our entrepreneurs report they have serious reservations about their ability to accomplish the tasks for which they are now training.

But if the entrepreneur's experience of being controlled by outside forces does not cause him to be insecure, what does? Actually, it appears that it is his prepotent power orientation—his need for expressing power, his need to affect others, his need to control others, and his need to enhance his own reputation—that is the most significant cause of his insecurity. His own demonstration of power is what worries him.

The regression analysis found in Figure 6.1 indicates that the entrepreneur's fear of other powerful people (and their potential control over him), coupled with a lack of personal control, cause the entrepreneur to be insecure.[6] It is not his feeling of being unable to master his fate (whole locus of control scores did not figure prominently in the insecurity of our entrepreneurs).

This finding, that the entrepreneur is insecure primarily because he

Table 6.3: Entrepreneurial Man: His Levels of Self-Esteem and Locus of Control

Group	Self-Esteem				Locus of Control*			
	N	$\bar{X}$	t	p value	N	$\bar{X}$	t	p value
1. Entrepreneurial Man	45	60.06 (SD = 5.68)			45	12.72 (SD = 2.38)		
2. Rational Man	43	84.91 (SD = 3.10)	25.28	.001	43	4.09 (SD = 1.52)	−20.10	.001
3. Existential Man	22	83.99 (SD = 3.57)	18.03	.001	22	11.50 (SD = 1.50)	2.19	.03
4. Administrative Man	23	61.82 (SD = 4.15)	1.46	.15	23	4.45 (SDD = 1.11)	−15.71	.001
5. Whole Business Elite	60	74.24 (SD = 9.34)	9.00	.001	60	7.59 (SD = 3.35)	8.66	.001
6. Whole Military Elite	223	75.35 (SD = 9.04)	9.04	.001	205	7.47 (SD = 3.46)	9.65	.001

*The two separable dimensions of "locus of control" were also disaggregated and compared for mean differences. When compared with the whole business and military populations, entrepreneurs score lower on both dimensions. The two dimensions are "personal control" (or the perceived ability to control one's feelings, emotions, and actions) and "system control" (or the perceived ability to control one's environment). Results of the two t tests are as follows: (1) personal control: business group, $t = 4.67$, $p < .001$; military group, $t = 7.55$, $p < .001$; (2) system control: business group, $t = 2.50$, $p < .001$; military group, $t = 4.65$, $p < .001$.

Figure 6.1: The Relative Influences of the Need for Power, Locus of Control, and Personal Control on the Insecurity of the Entrepreneur

	Regression coefficient
The Need for Power	.74 (p < .001)
The Experience of External Control	.14 ⟶ INSECURITY
Personal Control	.33 (p < .07)

$R^2 = 43.9$ (p. < .05).

fears the power of others and not because he fears he has a lack of ability to master his fate, is significant for three reasons. First, it represents a major departure from the personality dynamics of the classic Weberian entrepreneur; second, it shows that an external sense of control need not be the cause of insecurity as the locus of control literature has long maintained; and third, it provides the entrepreneur with a reaction formation that differs from that predicted by Weber.

THE SOURCE OF OUR ENTREPRENEUR'S UNHAPPINESS

The entrepreneur is uncertain of his ability to achieve continued success in the organization (though he is by all objective measures a "success");[7] he is uncertain of his personal capabilities and, unlike the classic Weberian man, he exudes a general sense of alienation, meaninglessness, and, even at times, despair. The joint effects of low self-esteem and the experience of being controlled by outside forces contribute to this leader's sense of detachment. Over 25 percent of the entrepreneurial group feel so discouraged with themselves that they "often" wonder whether it is all worth the effort (see Table 6.4).

This questioning of whether it is all worthwhile informs our understanding of the way in which this leader experiences his world. This sense of doubt is especially significant when we consider that our group of entrepreneurs have by all objective standards achieved success in American society. These are not people experiencing classical forms of alienation. The source of their discontent must be found in the more subjective realm of the senses.

Table 6.4: "Do you ever feel so discouraged with yourself that you wonder whether anything is worthwhile?" (%)

Group	N	Often	Not Very Often	Infrequently	Never
1. Entrepreneurial Man	45	26.7	42.2	28.9	2.2
2. Rational Man	43	2.3	9.3	32.6	53.5
3. Existential Man	22	0.0	18.2	45.5	36.5
4. Administrative Man	23	8.7	34.8	47.8	8.7
5. Whole Business Elite	61	4.9	34.4	37.7	23.0
6. Whole Military Elite	226	3.1	22.6	46.9	25.7

$X^2 = 55.26$, p. $< .001$ (Groups 1 through 4).
$X^2 = 68.64$, p. $< .001$ (Groups 1, 5, and 6).

THE ENTREPRENEUR EXPERIENCES LIFE AS A TRIAL

That the entrepreneur often questions whether it is all worthwhile strongly suggests dissatisfaction with his work and his "place" in his organization. We do have evidence that this type of leader neither enjoys his work nor finds it meaningful. Over 25 percent do not enjoy themselves on a typical work day, and when compared with our other leaders more than twice as many entrepreneurs report doing their work out of a sense of duty (see Table 6.5).

The experience of external control does not cause insecurity as we know it, but a lack of optimism and hope. Unlike the Weberian entrepreneur, who believes that his actions can affect his place in eternity, our entrepreneur feels dispair. It is the consistent direction and perhaps not the magnitude of our findings that is of significance. Tables 6.4 and 6.5 show that the entrepreneur both enjoys his work significantly less than the two parent population groups and at the same time more often feels so discouraged that he wonders whether anything is worthwhile.

MOTIVATIONAL DETERMINANTS

Our entrepreneurial man has been portrayed as insecure and uncertain; his motivational system as measured through thematic apperception lends support to this characterization. His projective imagery indicates that as a group, he shows both the least need for achievement, the greatest need for personal power, and, most critically, the greatest inhibition. (The inhibition or self-control component ensures the "future orientation" of the classic entrepreneur. Such a man must be capable of investing in his future and deferring immediate gratifications for the sake of long-term rewards.) The combinatorial pattern displayed in Table 6.6 is highly congruent with the pattern exhibited by Weber's entrepreneur. Not all of the findings reach conventional levels of statistical significance, but again, the evidence is cumulative and offers a consistent, cohesive characterological pattern.

Compared with the (whole) sample of business and military leaders, the entrepreneurial man shows little direct concern with achieving according to ideal standards in solving challenging problems. Neither solving problems nor achieving in the traditional sense provides this leader with a sense of accomplishment. But this leader does have very strong power needs, and like the classic entrepreneur, his need for power is primarily "personalized" (for our entrepreneur, need for power and its "personalized" component have an r of .62, p < .001). This means that the

Table 6.5: "How much do you enjoy yourself on a typical work day?" (%)

Group	N	Very Much	Much	Not so Much
1. Entrepreneurial Man	45	11.1	62.2	26.7
2. Rational Man	43	58.1	41.9	0.0
3. Existential Man	22	45.5	45.5	9.0
4. Administrative Man	23	21.7	60.9	17.4
5. Whole Business Elite	61	31.1	62.3	6.5
6. Whole Military Elite	225	25.3	58.2	15.4

$X^2 = 30.62$, p. $< .001$ (Groups 1 through 4).
$X^2 = 11.39$, p. $< .03$ (Groups 1, 5, and 6).

Table 6.6: Entrepreneurial Man: His Need for Achievement and Power and His Level of Inhibition

Group	N	Need Achievement			Need Power			Personal Power			Inhibition		
		$\bar{X}$	t	p value	$\bar{X}$	t	p value	$\bar{X}$	t	p value	$\bar{X}$	t	p value
1. Entrepreneurial Man	38	2.16 (SD = 4.68)			3.75 (SD = 3.57)			0.66 (SD = 0.74)			1.67 (SD = 3.09)		
2. Rational Man	38	3.83 (SD = 4.34)	1.60	.11	2.78 (SD = 3.95)	−1.11	NS	0.32 (SD = 0.74)	−1.94	.05	1.07 (SD = 2.09)	−0.98	NS
3. Existential Man	22	2.55 (SD = 4.49)	0.28	NS	4.09 (SD = 4.31)	0.26	NS	0.35 (SD = 0.74)	−1.29	NS	0.88 (SD = 1.79)	−1.13	NS
4. Administrative Man	16	5.53 (SD = 4.21)	2.60	.01	1.69 (SD = 2.50)	−2.37	.02	0.33 (SD = 0.81)	−1.34	.19	1.15 (SD = 1.46)	−0.62	NS
5. Whole Business Elite	49	2.22 (SDD = 4.56)	−0.06	NS	3.28 (SD = 3.97)	0.58	NS	0.28 (SD = 0.57)	2.54	.01	1.07 (SD = 1.84)	1.05	NS
6. Whole Military Elite	182	4.03 (SD = 4.44)	2.25	.03	2.73 (SD = 3.39)	1.61	.11	0.39 (SD = 0.71)	1.97	.05	1.06 (SD = 1.81)	1.62	.10

entrepreneur is driven by an explicit concern with impacting others and at the same time a fear of losing power to others. This fear is consistent with our representation of the entrepreneur as one who mistrusts others.

The need for the enrichment of personal power is consistent with (although not identical to) that of Weber's entrepreneur. He too was motivated by an explicit concern with enhancing his own reputation or boosting his symbolic sense of self-worth. While the classic entrepreneur enhances his worth through the accumulation of monetary wealth, we will hypothesize that the organizational entrepreneur would enhance his worth through the accumulation of organizational wealth (prestige, status, and power). But we must defer our test of this hypothesis until the second part of the chapter.

Our entrepreneurial man, despite his need for power, is highly inhibited. Unlike the existential leader, who is apt to live out his fantasies of power, the entrepreneur restrains direct expression of his power needs and maintains self-control through self-discipline. As we have mentioned, the inhibition component of the entrepreneur's need system is critical. Weber maintained that the man who was both insecure and unable to control his fate was inhibited. But what Weber did not maintain was that inhibition would promote social withdrawal and a disposition toward professional quietism. The apparent failing of Weber's theory was his inability to recognize that inhibition causes internalization and repression of power needs (and the activist impulse), rather than externalization and activity. Weber underestimated the pervasiveness of the superego.

MOTIVES AND WORLD VIEW

A glance at the kinds of stories our entrepreneurial man writes in response to the TAT protocols contributes to our portrayal of this leader as essentially an unhappy fatalist. Note the recurrence of themes expressing doubt, hope and yearning rather than firm expectation, lack of fulfillment, disappointment, and a general lack of positive affect:

1. *Park Bench Picture* (Figure 6.2)

> The couple are lovers and have had a quarrel. The girl is the injured party and judging by the plaintive look on the man's face, I'd say he is *trying* to apologize. Right now, however, his apology is *falling on deaf ears*.

> ... the girl ... feels *resentment* due to some *disappointment* in her job. After several meetings, the girl tried to back out, but her (boss) would not allow that. The *gray of the sky matches her mood*.

Figure 6.2: "Park Bench"*

Just look at the picture briefly (10–15 seconds), turn the page, and write out the story it suggests.

*Source: D. C. McClelland and R. S. Steele, *Human Motivation Workshops*, 1972. Reprinted by permission of the senior author.

2. Women in Lab Picture (see Figure 4.1)

The two scientists have been working to isolate a virus. A *critical* experiment in nearing an outcome. They are *anxious* and *hoping* for success soon. The experiment was *inconclusive* and had to be redone.

The woman made a *mistake* and is redoing the experiment. The people are working to see if the experiment will be a success this time. Both are *feeling nervous* and *hoping* that it will be successful.

3. Ship's Captain Picture (Figure 6.3)

The admiral . . . is hoping to get funds through the congressmen's subcommittee. The congressman has shown *skepticism* and *doubts* the sincerity of the words he is hearing . . . the result is no funds, a disgruntled admiral, and a congressman *wondering* if he did the right thing.

Figure 6.3: "Ship's Captain"*

Just look at the picture briefly (10–15 seconds), turn the page, and write out the story it suggests.

*Source: D. C. McClelland, et al., *The Drinking Man*, 1972. Reprinted by permission of the senior author.

> The captain is trying *desperately* to persuade the (other party) that there is no truth to his allegation but he's *worried as hell*.

A content analysis of all TAT protocols brings into sharper focus the way in which the entrepreneurial man views himself and his world. In over 67 percent of all stories written by entrepreneurs, story outcomes were negative. As consistent with his perception of being controlled by extrinsic forces, the entrepreneur frequently portrays characters who express feelings of uncertainty. As predicted by his need for personal power, the entrepreneur shows concern with hierarchic relations (his "place" in the scheme of things), while over 20 percent of the stories written by entrepreneurial men portray characters who use force and hostility. And providing some convergent validity for our finding that entrepreneurial men score low on the self-esteem scale, our entrepreneur's TAT story characters show little self-confidence.

The data we have gathered thus far indicate a strong congruence between the personality dynamics of Weber's man and that of our own entrepreneur. As Weber predicted, inhibition marks the man who is uncertain of his fate. And, too, our entrepreneur experiences a world view much like that of Weber's man—imposing, threatening, and uncertain.

Our entrepreneur displays a motive dispositional system that comes very close to what McClelland (1976) has called the system of the "empire builder"—high in need power, low in the need for affiliation, and high in inhibition. It is obvious that the appellation empire builder could also be used to describe the quintessential (Protestant) American entrepreneur. The Morgans and the Rockefellers were empire builders. The strong need for prestige, power, personal recognition, and stature, coupled with what social scientists would describe as an imposing superego (which demands self-control and a disciplined, goal-directed channeling of energy) together with weak social approval needs, is believed by Weber and McClelland to produce entrepreneurial, or empire-building, behavior.

Weber believed that the motive system we have been describing was cultivated by a sense of doubt and the experience of being controlled by outside forces. These are central characteristics of our entrepreneur. What remains to be demonstrated is the alleged causal connection between his motive system and entrepreneurial behavior. This is the task of the following section of this chapter.

THE ENTREPRENEUR AS SELF-STARTER

Weber's thesis asserts that the exogenously controlled, low self-esteem entrepreneur would be bold, somehow capable of suppressing his control-related anxieties and able to take the necessary risks associated with innovation. In short, Weber would predict that our entrepreneur would be highly activistic and motivated to take initiatives. Weber's theory asserts that ambiguity either about the self and its worth or about the self and the ability to control creates a level of anxiety that is the necessary psychological precondition for initiative taking or attempts at innovation. We must now test this assertion by ascertaining whether our entrepreneur feels compelled to take initiatives as a strategy to gain power (the "currency" of every leader), or whether his sense of anxiety is debilitating in nature, producing professional quietism and personal withdrawal.

While our entrepreneur has a distinct need to enhance his reputation, he is not especially aggressive or assertive.[8] He is essentially inhibited, and this inhibition interferes with, or attentuates the acting out of, his desire for prestige. The entrepreneur does not attempt to affect other people in order to satisfy his desire for prestige, for his power needs are tempered by some inner impulse that demands moderation (psychologists like to call this impulse the superego). As Tables 6.7 and 6.8 illustrate, the basic personality configuration of our entrepreneur leads him to withdraw from initiative taking when such behavior is people-oriented in nature.

Because the entrepreneur feels he is the object of forces outside him, because he fears and mistrusts others, and because he is essentially an inhibited man, it is no surprise that he rarely takes initiatives when they require stimulating the ambitions or motivations of others or otherwise enhancing the performance of people he regards as potential rivals. To stimulate the ambitions of others would be contrary to one of his most fundamental personality needs. The entrepreneur fears others; he does not try to empower them.

Like the Weberian entrepreneur, who was a loner and not a socialized bureaucrat, our entrepreneur shies away from interaction with his associates. His inhibition prevents the acting out of his purely personal power drive. Because he fears others and because he is inhibited, the entrepreneur tends toward withdrawal. Rather than seeking control of his environment as did the classic Weberian entrepreneur, our entrepreneur turns within. He does not present superiors with recommendations unless they are expressly solicited, and he does not gravitate toward or otherwise come to acquire visible positions of command.

Our entrepreneur is not a leader of men but a manager. His initiative taking, like that of Whyte's (1956) administrative man, is process-oriented and not people-oriented. Whether it be because his superiors perceive that the entrepreneur mistrusts them and thus find him difficult to work with, or because he is not attracted to visible positions of power, the entrepreneur refrains from a posture of command. Much like Maccoby's (1976) "craftsman" he may seek to build a "bigger and better mousetrap," but he does not have the will to lead other men. His ethos may be acquisitive, but it does not involve the domination of others.

The Weber theory asserts that the entrepreneur is the product of unique cultural conditions. He is one who is somehow willing, or somehow by inner compulsion, able to take the risk that will enhance his worth and eliminate his sense of doubt. The Weber thesis therefore predicts that the entrepreneur will not only be a frequent seeker of challenges but also one who creates challenges. He is singularly adept at exploiting the confluence of situational circumstances that others would ignore and that could make him a more powerful, *worthy* man.

Again, however, our data directly contradict the Weber thesis.

Table 6.7: "I try to stimulate the ambition of my associates" (%)

Group	N	Always	Very Often	Often	Not Very Often
1. Entrepreneurial Man	45	6.7	61.2	31.2	0.0
2. Rational Man	43	41.9	48.8	4.7	2.3
3. Existential Man	22	36.4	59.1	4.5	0.0
4. Administrative Man	23	8.7	69.6	21.7	0.0
5. Whole Business Elite	61	29.5	62.3	6.6	0.0
6. Whole Military Elite	225	21.7	62.8	11.9	1.7

$X^2 = 28.72$, p. $< .001$ (Group 1 through 4).
$X^2 = 17.31$, p. $< .005$ (Groups 1, 5, and 6).

Table 6.8: Entrepreneurial Man: The Relationship Between His Personality and People-Oriented Initiative-Taking Behavior (N = 44) (Pearson correlation coefficients)

	Presents Superiors with Unsolicited Recommendations	Stimulates Ambitions of Associates
External Experience of Control	−.10 (NS)	−.33 $p < .01$
Inhibition	−.30 $p < .03$	−.15 (NS)
Fear of Powerful Others	.01 (NS)	−.27 $p < .05$
Mistrust of Others	−.26 $p < .04$	−.20 $p < .09$

Evidence (in the form of self-reports) reveals that leaders who are both insecure and unable to experience control do not seek challenges as often as do their more secure cohorts. They seem not to be intrinsically motivated to create challenges, but rather they respond to challenges that routinely cross their desk (see Tables 6.9 and 6.10).

The entrepreneur, contrary to the Weber thesis, chooses not to grapple with the risk associated with initiative taking. He does not in any way feel compelled to personally seek out challenges or actively to create challenges. When he does have the compulsion, his inhibition prevents him from acting on it. The entrepreneur is unable to create challenges because he does not have confidence that these challenges will be met successfully. Our evidence indicates that the joint effects of low self-esteem and the sense of being controlled by outside forces promote not the activistic orientation of Weber's entrepreneur but an orientation of comparative social quietism.

What is apparently critical for the nurturance of an initiative taking impulse is a sense of personal efficacy. The entrepreneur does not believe in himself and his leadership capabilities. His strong sense of personal insecurity and his lack of self-esteem promote passive resignation to the forces that act upon him and those that are beyond his control. Unlike Weber's man, he does not harbor a compulsion to act. His sense of being controlled, more often than not, results in the internalization of his anxieties. Unlike the classic leader of men, he does not externalize his needs and seek control of the forces that act against him. His behavior does not appear to be compensatory in nature.

In short, the men both Weber and I have called "entrepreneurs" are not the most entrepreneurial people among business and military elites. Weber's entrepreneur, it turns out, lives in a world that he experiences as a Hobbesian jungle—fearful, alone, mistrustful of others and his own creative instincts, and scared of becoming the victim of other powerful people. Such an individual is clearly unable to use effectively his own abilities and skills for the creation of new enterprises.

Weber was wrong. Inhibited, insecure, worried people are not motivated to accept and create new challenges. These people shy away from challenges and worry that where they will fail, others will succeed. That he deals in a threatening zero-sum world makes the entrepreneur an unlikely candidate to be the "transformative principle" in the move from premodern to modern forms of corporate organization. He appears not to be the type to usher in new forms of rationalism, for the insecure, inhibited person is more likely to be an emotional rather than rational man. Emotional men are unable to acquire and practice the bold, assertive, and dispassionate style of the true entrepreneur.

Table 6.9: "How often do you actively go out and seek challenges?" (%)

Group	N	Always	Very Often	Often	Not very often/Not at all
1. Entrepreneurial Man	45	2.2	26.7	48.9	22.2
2. Rational Man	43	25.6	46.5	23.3	4.6
3. Existential Man	22	17.8	64.2	17.8	0.0
4. Administrative Man	23	0.0	26.1	47.8	26.0
5. Whole Business Elite	61	11.5	60.7	24.6	3.3
6. Whole Military Elite	226	8.4	39.4	37.2	14.6

$X^2 = 40.14$, p. $< .001$ (Groups 1 through 4).
$X^2 = 22.48$, p. $< .001$ (Groups 1, 5, and 6).

137

Table 6.10: "Would you consider yourself a person who actively looks for challenges or someone who becomes motivated primarily through challenges that appear on your desk?" (%)

Group	N	"I actively look for challenges"	"... that appear on desk"
1. Entrepreneurial Man	45	51.1	48.9
2. Rational Man	43	86.0	9.3
3. Existential Man	22	90.0	9.0
4. Administrative Man	23	52.2	47.8
5. Whole Business Elite	61	82.0	16.4
6. Whole Military Elite	220	75.7	21.7

$X^2 = 23.80$, p. $< .001$ (Groups 1 through 4).
$X^2 = 16.96$, p. $< .001$ (Groups 1, 5, and 6).

HEDONISM: THE WEBERIAN IMPERATIVE

The classic entrepreneur pursues wealth in a vigorously rational manner. His inhibition and his need to prove his worth frame a posture of what Weber has called, "this worldly asceticism." Asceticism may be thought of as the antithesis of hedonism.

In order for us to test the hypothesis that entrepreneurs are ascetic we asked our respondents, "If as a young man you had inherited a great fortune, would you have pursued your present career?—if not, what would you have done?" (See Table 6.11.) Our expectation was that the true entrepreneur was driven by a "calling"—the need to work as an end in itself and as fulfillment of his worldly obligations. If indeed the entrepreneur was imbued with the Protestant ethic he should say, "Yes, I would have pursued my present career," or he would choose another professional pursuit as demanding as his present one. He would not, we reasoned, choose to spend his life in a hedonistic manner, spending frivolously his good fortune. This would be counter to the ascetic ethos of the classic entrepreneur. Again, our evidence contradicts what the Weber thesis would predict. Entrepreneurial men show no special propensity for pursuing careers consistent with the Protestant ethic. They would choose careers much the same as their corporate executive cohorts.

Of the 60 percent of our entrepreneurs who would not have pursued their present careers, only about one-quarter would have sought vocations consistent with the Protestant ethic. Of these, many said they would have owned their own businesses, and quite a few would have chosen to be lawyers, physicians, or engineers. A small number would have been writers or involved themselves in the performing arts or "humanistic goals." About one-fifth of the group would have led what could be called a

Table 6.11: "If you had inherited a great fortune as a young man, would you have pursued your present career?" (%)

Group	N	Yes	No
1. Entrepreneurial Man	45	37.8	60.0
2. Rational Man	39	41.9	48.8
3. Existential Man	22	31.8	68.2
4. Administrative Man	22	43.5	52.2
5. Whole Business Elite	61	32.8	60.7
6. Whole Military Elite	(NO DATA)		

$X^2 = 1.38$, NS (Groups 1 through 4).
$X^2 = 0.58$, NS (Groups 1 and 5).

hedonistic existence. One man claimed he would seek adventure through car racing, one would merely "sit back and enjoy," two others would just "spend money," and one openly proclaimed he would lead a purely "hedonistic" life.

But our other corporate executives tell very similar stories. A little less than half would have pursued their present careers, and of those who would not have, most would have gone into other professions. We can offer little evidence in support of Weber's assertion that the entrepreneur is a true ascetic. The business elite as a class apparently have internalized the Protestant ethic. These are people who enjoy or otherwise need to work as professionals.

OVERVIEW OF THE ENTREPRENEURIAL MAN

There are few objective methods that we may utilize in ascertaining whether our entrepreneur has pursued organizational power more intensely than his colleagues. Because, however, the Weber theory maintains that the entrepreneur labors intensely as an end in itself, there is a theoretically compelling reason why this should be so. While we have assessed the need structure of our entrepreneurial man and concluded that he does have a strong concern with protecting and expanding his organizational base of power, it does not necessarily follow that he acts toward the attainment of that end as much as do other leaders. The entrepreneur, as we have said, is a highly inhibited man.

Inhibition acts to suppress this leader's urge to take initiatives. While he does desire the accumulation of power, by his own admission (and when compared with our other leaders) he does not act toward that end. It is likely that our entrepreneur fears reprisals from powerful others and this fear effectively militates against the taking of initiatives. More than either of our two parent populations as a whole, the entrepreneur believes that "ambitious people create enemies."

Our entrepreneur tempers his needs. While our other leaders (essentially uninhibited men) act out their strivings for power, the entrepreneur suppresses and even restructures his strivings. This process is a function of the superego. Because the entrepreneur cannot and does not, directly and freely act to satisfy his most desired personality need (that of power), we may infer that he is essentially unfulfilled, and from the data we have presented we may infer that this type of leader does not pursue power more intensely than do his colleagues.

Our entrepreneur is the type of man who is most likely to acquire anonymous power, or that type of power that can be exercised behind the scenes. He has neither the "expectancy of success" nor the "command identity" of other types of leaders. He has neither the disposition nor the temperament to be a classic "entrepreneurial" leader of men.

THE PERSONALITY CHARACTERISTICS OF THE ENTREPRENEUR: MULTISTUDY CONVERGENCES

A review of the literature shows that there have been at least seven major studies of entrepreneurs: Weber (1958), Schumpeter (1934), Hagen (1962), Collins, Moore, and Unwalla (1964), Spranger (1966), Zalesnik and deVries (1975), and McClelland (1976). Twenty personality characteristics have been attributed to entrepreneurs in the present study. All 20 have been discussed in at least one of the seven major studies of entrepreneurs, and most have been discussed in three or more of these works.

Multistudy convergences of findings are illustrated in Table 6.12. To date, these findings represent our knowledge of the "entrepreneurial" personality. Fifteen of the 20 personality characteristics attributed to entrepreneurs in the present study were also attributed to entrepreneurs in two or more of the other studies. These studies are supportive of our findings that entrepreneurs are personally insecure, inhibited, alienated, distrustful of others, high in the need for power, unfulfilled, uncertain, skeptical, nonhedonistic, and anxiety-ridden. They also feel that their fate is exogenously determined; they perceive the world as threatening and they fear other powerful people.

One study (Hagen) asserts that entrepreneurs have "freedom from doubt" while four (including the present study) disagree with that assertion. Another (McClelland) maintains that entrepreneurs enjoy their work while five of the studies, including the present one, present evidence to the contrary. Two (Zalesnik and deVries, and Hagen) claim that entrepreneurs have a need for social approval, though three disagree, and the same two authors believe that entrepreneurs show an interest in groups while only the present study maintains otherwise.

There are two points at which the findings of the present work and that of some of the others diverge. The first point concerns the entrepreneur and his need to achieve; the second is concerned with the alleged impulse toward activity that is said to characterize the entrepreneur. Our TAT analysis has shown that relative to other elite organizational leaders entrepreneurs have weak achievement needs. Their primary motivation is not to achieve, but to prove their self-worth and overcome their sense of fear.[9] The act of achieving we considered a means to this less easily satisfied end. McClelland (1976 :265) supports our contention when he states,

Table 6.12: Personality Characteristics of the Entrepreneur: Convergences of Findings in Eight Studies (cont.)

This Study	Weber	McClelland	Spranger	Hagen	Zalesnik and deVries	Shumpeter	Collins, Moore and Unwalla
Doubtful	X			Freedom from doubt	Injured self-esteem		
Personally insecure	X			"Self-trusting"	Feelings of powerlessness		X
Exogenous control (social and personal)	X				X		Strong need for control
Inhibited	X	X					
Distantiated/Alienated	Is a loner			Detachment from society/apathy	X		
Mistrustful (of superiors and subordinates)					X		X
High "personalized" power orientation	X	X	Strong need for power/egotistical		Strong need to be admired	Will to conquer/impulse to fight/egotistical	Need to dominate others

142

	Fear of separation	Need for social approval	Regards welfare of groups / Strong need for nurturance / Strong need for achievement	Shows little interest in others / Highly competitive	Strong need for achievement	Enjoys work	Persistent feelings of dissatisfaction	Indifference to enjoyment / Does not enjoy labor	Sense of disillusion-ment
Low "socialized" power orientation									
Weak need for affiliation — Weak social approval needs									
Weak need for achievement — Strong need for achievement									
Uncertain — Ascribes no intrinsic satisfaction to work — Unfulfilled	X								
Lack of positive affect									
Skeptical	X							X	
Non-Hedonistic	X								X

Table 6.12: Personality Characteristics of the Entrepreneur: Convergences of Findings in Eight Studies (cont.)

This Study	Weber	McClelland	Spranger	Hagen	Zalesnik and deVries	Shumpeter	Collins, Moore and Unwalla
Perception of world as imposing/threatening				X			
Fears powerful others	X				X		X
Anxiety-ridden					X		
Passive	Highly active	Active/adaptive	Highly active	High energy level			
Moderately acquisitive	Highly acquisitive	X	Highly acquisitive				
	Self-disciplined	X		X		Seeks change for the sake of change	Shows restlessness
	Rational	X	Views world as capable of being understood	X		Non-rational except in pursuit of utility	Shows self-control
	Able to defer gratifications	Pragmatic	X			Enjoys getting things done	
		Respect for institutional authority					

	Willingness to submit to higher authority	Willingness to take a risk
Moderate risk-taker		
Strong sense of duty	X	
Strong need for autonomy	X	
Feelings of guilt		
Rigidity		
Imaginative		
Conflicts of indentifi-tion		
Defensive structure		
Instability of attitudes		
Psychological deprivation		
Seeks out difficult situations		
No clearly envisaged goals		

> ...for years people have been mistakenly interpreting my studies of achievement motivation as meaning that people with high n Achievement represent the Protestant work ethic. They don't. They like to do things more efficiently and get out of work. Apparently it is people with high n Power, low n Affiliation and high control (inhibition) who like to work for its own sake because it is a form of self-discipline.

High need for power, low need for affiliation, and inhibition are all salient features of the group of leaders we have called entrepreneurial men. Achieving behavior, therefore, seems not to be a primary personality disposition, but a reaction formation arising out of the need to satisfy other more compelling drives.

While entrepreneurs are known by definition as energetic corporate organizers, we have found that when compared with other leaders they are relatively passive. Our evidence contravenes several other studies and, of course, the Weber thesis itself. Stanislaw Andreski (1968: 54), in a piece that is highly supportive of the Weber thesis, has said,

> The weakest point in the (Weber) argument ... is the assertion linking predestination with the acquisitive drive. It is difficult to see how an earnest belief that one's fate is determined by something absolutely beyond one's control could stimulate anybody to exert himself. Fatalism ... is generally considered to be one of the greatest obstacles to economic development ... It appears therefore that this tenet ... provided neither stimulus not obstacle to the growth of capitalism.

The evidence presented here supports Andreski's intuitive argument and leads us to conclude that insecure, inhibited men who experience the belief that their fate is somehow predetermined or otherwise affected by forces outside their control are uneasy or somehow unfulfilled, but they are not, as a result, unusually activistic. Their fear of other powerful people and their general experience of insecurity prevents them from taking the bold risk, the fortuitous initiative or the unpopular but profitable decision that characterizes the true entrepreneur. Weber was aware of the gnawing effects of self-doubt, but he was unaware of its debilitating consequences. Self-doubt does not stimulate one to conquer the world, but to withdraw from it.

CONCLUSION

There exists a type of leader who is essentially insecure, inhibited, mistrusting, fearful of power, and detached from the ethos of his organization. Such a leader is not an entrepreneur in the classic Weberian tradition. He neither feels compelled to take action, nor is he able to bear the risks associated with innovation. This type of leader is, in effect, not a leader at all, but a manager.

Our test of Weber's thesis does not support his main contention—that low self-esteem and feelings of incomplete control cause or contribute to the formation of an ascetic, acquisitive, and activistic personality. We have not, of course, settled the controversy generated by the *Protestant Ethic and the Spirit of Capitalism*, but we do have strong evidence that the Weber thesis is too broadly drawn. People attempt to work out their insecurities and prove their self-worth through behavior that need not be of an entrepreneurial or even professional nature. It is apparent that Weber underestimated the power of the superego and the multiplicity of ways in which it can affect human behavior.

NOTES

1. *Webster's Dictionary.* For a good discussion of the historical roles of entrepreneurs see John W. Atkinson and B. F. Hoselitz, "Entrepreneurship and Personality," in *Explorations in Entrepreneurial History,* 1958, 10 pp. 107–112. The authors maintain that historically the entrepreneur has had three major roles: risk bearing, managing, and innovating.

2. Weber (1958: 63) believed that asceticism, together with mental concentration and a feeling of obligation to one's job, "provides the most favorable foundation for the concentration of labor as an end in itself, as a calling which is necessary to capitalism . . . "

3. Weber (1958: 54) states, "We are interested in . . . the influence of those psychological sanctions that, originating in religious belief and the practice of religion, gave a direction to practical conduct and held the individual to it."

4. It is important to point out a generic difference between our entrepreneur and that of Weber, that is, his economic relationship with the organization. While our entrepreneurs are salaried by large bureaucracies, the classic entrepreneur was said to operate in the small-business profit-motive milieu.

5. There is no reason for us to believe that there should be (objective) systematic differences with respect to IQ betweeen the entrepreneurial man and the whole group of corporate and military elites. Both self-esteem and locus of control have been found to be unrelated to conventional measures of intelligence. Self-estimates of IQ were measured through use of a semantic differential.

6. The regression equation contained eight independent personality variables. These were the three variables in Figure 6.1, need for affiliation, need for personal power, fear of power, locus of control, and interpersonal trust. All variables but locus of control and trust were measured through TAT analysis.

7. Among the group of entrepreneurial men, we find two assistant general managers, five directors and general managers, two full colonels and fourteen lieutenant colonels.

8. On our semantic differential measure of "activity-passivity" mean differences between the entrepreneur and the whole business and military populations do not reach conventional levels of significance (two-tailed t test).

9. Consistent with the writings of Lasswell (1930, 1948, 1965) we have shown that entrepreneurial power seeking is a compensatory behavior.

CHAPTER 7

SELF-ESTEEM AND INSECURITY
IN LEADERS AND MANAGERS

FOUR PORTRAITS: THE INTERCONNECTEDNESS OF CHARACTER, WORLD VIEW, AND BEHAVIOR

The typology developed in this work stresses the logical flow from character to world view to behavior. Our supposition has been that each of the four leadership types has a uniquely different personality, hence a uniquely different vision and experience of the organization. By mapping the internal states of mind of the four leadership types, we have traced the genesis of four world views, each a lens through which all incoming information is filtered, interpreted, and understood. These world views are the central axes around which our four types revolve and help us to understand why each leader has a different "style," why each tries to influence the organization in different ways and for different purposes, and why each strives for power and social recognition.

THE "MAN IN THE LEADER": THE RELATIONSHIP BETWEEN PERSONALITY AND BEHAVIOR

Neither an understanding of a leader's image of himself, nor an understanding of a leader's image of the world can create for us a full picture of what Lucian Pye (1976) has called "the man in the leader." We need to understand how the leader views himself and how he views the world. We must then systematically relate this knowledge to the way the leader acts in his world.

The relationship between personality and leadership is extraordinarily complex. In recognizing this complexity Aaron Wildavsky recently referred to the concept of leadership as a "disappearing act." It is worth quoting Wildavsky (1980: 51) at length:

> Just as all roads used to lead to Rome, all paths to the study of leadership end up by swallowing their subject matter. In the beginning, there were thought to be self-evident leaders who shared certain physical or psychological traits. They were taller and heavier and had a drive to dominance. After much effort, it was generally agreed that the enterprise was ill-conceived, partly because leaders stubbornly refused to show common traits, but mostly because of the realization that there could be no leaders without followers. Exit the heroes and enter the masses. Alas, followers were even more diverse than leaders. Of course! There had to be an oversight. Leaders and followers were related by something, and that something was the situation. Yet situations, it turned out . . . were more varied than followers, who were more diverse than leaders. By socializing leadership, by merging leaders with followers and folding them both into situations, leadership has disappeared into society.

While much of what Wildavsky says does reverberate with the ring of truth, his despair seems a bit excessive. What appears to be the "disappearing" of leadership is really the painful recognition that leadership cannot be easily reduced to elegant scientific laws either about personality or situation. Leadership is the particular combination of both, with such added unpredictables as mood, will, passion, and cultural milieu. But surely acts of leadership are carried out for particular reasons and with particular intentions. The process is not random, nor does it necessarily have to be swallowed up, as Wildavsky suggests, by some kind of whirlpool of failed knowledge.

LEADERS AND MANAGERS

Some of the best-known and most prosaic characterizations of leaders have excellent face validity and are aided by good clinical interpretation, yet they purposefully mitigate the complexity and variability of the constellation of personality and structural factors that drive behavior. Take Plato's men of silver, iron, or brass. Or Riesman's (1950) inner and other directed types. Or Machiavelli's lions and foxes. If Machiavelli were to say that Cesare Borgia, the reigning leader of his time was a lion, but he was a fox when a certain general sought more troops for the invasion of Bologna, and a snake when he had his troops kill Messer Remirro de Orca in his sleep, and a fish when Lady Borgia asked for more furs, the reader would think Borgia not a lion, but some kind of platypus—not the kind of typological image one such as Machiavelli would evoke. Such an image would not have lasted almost five centuries.

In truth, Machiavelli's famous general was not pure lion but was indeed a platypus. Perhaps on the day of the battle he was a true lion, and perhaps in the company of his troops he was a lion. But at other times and in other places Borgia displayed characteristics foreign to kings of the jungle. Likewise, Riesman and his colleagues may have found certain people to be "other-directed" with respect to their politics, but perhaps "inner-directed" with regard to their work. Attaching an endless array of qualifications to a typology renders the typology confusing and less vivid. More often than not, it will also detract from the mutual exclusivity of its parts.

It is not that Plato, Machiavelli, and other typologizers are being necessarily simplistic, it is that we all have a fondness for breaking down the complex into the simple, for stereotyping and categorizing. As Greenstein has stated in *Personality and Politics* (1975: 94): "The process of abstracting common features from diverse individual phenomena and classifying the *types* of regularities that one confronts is possibly as fundamental as any aspect of cognitive functioning (Greenstein's italics)."

Our own study suggested that not all powerholders are alike. The motivations and intentions of people we classified as leaders differ markedly from those we identified as managers. Their respective views of the world differ, the ways in which they interact with subordinates differ, and in all probability, the life histories of the two types differ.[1] Yet the differences that mark those who lead from those who simply maintain the status quo are not all too bold but are rather subtle and make difficult any attempt to typologize the two.[2] Nevertheless, by more formally distinguishing between leaders and managers we may be able to understand better the psychological dynamics that underlie the pursuit of power.

DIMENSIONS OF LEADERS' PERSONALITITES: MATCHING THE FOUR TYPES TO LEVINSON'S CRITERIA FOR CHOOSING CHIEF EXECUTIVE OFFICERS

In a well-known and much discussed article published in the *Harvard Business Review*, Harry Levinson (1980) presents 20 criteria that should be used by companies in judging the capabilities of prospective chief executive officers. Levinson distilled these specific criteria from among the hundreds of qualities exhibited by executives he has studied over the last several years.

While we do not endeavor to use the typology presented in this work as a clinical tool by which organizational leaders may be evaluated and recruited, we may be able, by use of Levinson's schema, to provide some external validity to our suggestion that rational and existential men are best suited for positions of leadership, while administrators and entrepreneurs are more dispositionally suited for managerial roles. We then can go on to extrapolate from our specific findings and provide a more general theory about the psychological qualities that distinguish leaders from managers.

Scoring Levinson's Schema

Scoring of Levinson's schema consisted of matching each of our types to all 20 criteria and assigning each a rank between "+++" and "−." The symbol "+" indicates a positive match on the part of the type being evaluated, and the symbol "−" indicates that the leadership type would not do well on that dimension. Empirical data are not always available in scoring each of our leaders on Levinson's criteria, so in several instances we have drawn inferences based either on limited indirect data gathered in this work or from other research on the qualities endemic to the types.[3] Criteria that were scored inferentially are indicated with an asterisk.

Findings

Rational men score very highly on dimensions that measure their capacity to abstract and conceptualize information, their ability to be practical, their general activity level, the degree to which they feel involved with the goals of the organization, their ability to persevere and stick to a task despite setbacks, their personal sense of organization and use of time, and their ability to use a well-established and previously tested value system. Rational men also score well on achievement orientation, sensitivity, their ability to deal adequately with other people's feelings, their ability to maintain healthy workable relationships with authority figures, and their sense of vision both with respect to their own careers and the organization as a whole. Rational men score less well on the remaining seven dimensions, yet they do not score negatively on a single item. If we total up rational man's number of positive matches to Levinson's criteria for choosing leaders, we would get a score of 40 points (see Table 7.1).

Existential men score very highly on dimensions that measure tolerance for ambiguity and the ability to tolerate confusion, constructive feelings of authority, their general level of activity and vigor with which they approach their job, the degree of physical as well as mental stamina they possess, their ability to be adaptable and capable of managing stress, and their general orientation toward perseverance. Existential men also do well on those criteria that measure their capacity to be abstract as well as practical, their feel for knowing when to act, their sense of achievement,

Table 7.1: Dimensions of Leaders' Personalities: Matching the Four Types with Levinson's Criteria for Choosing Chief Executives*

Criteria	Rational Man	Existential Man	Administrative Man	Entrepreneurial Man
Capacity to abstract, to conceptualize, to organize and to integrate different data into a coherent frame of reference*	+++	+	++	++
Tolerance for ambiguity; can stand confusion	+	+++	−	++
Intelligence; has the capacity not only to be abstract, but to be practical*	+++	++	+	++
Judgement; knows when to act*	+	++	++	+
Authority, has the feeling that he or she belongs in the boss's role	+	+++	−	+++
Activity, takes a vigorous orientation to problems and needs of the organization	+++	+++	+	+
Achievement, oriented towards organization's success rather than personal aggrandizement	++	++	+	−
Sensitivity, able to perceive subtleties of others' feelings*	++	+	+	−
Involvement, sees oneself as a participating member of the organization	+++	++	+++	+
Maturity, has good relationships with authority figures	++	+	−	−
Independence, accepts appropriate dependency needs of others as well as of him or herself	+	++	−	++
Articulateness, makes a good impression*	++	++	−	+
Stamina, has physical as well as mental energy	++	+++	+++	+++

Table 7.1 (continued)

Criteria	Rational Man	Existential Man	Administrative Man	Entrepreneurial Man
Adaptability, manages stress well	+	+++	–	++
Sense of humor, doesn't take self too seriously*	+	+	–	–
Vision, is clear about progression of his or her own life and career, as well as where the organization should go*	++	+	++	++
Perseverance, able to stick to a task and see it through regardless of the difficulties encountered	+++	+++	++	+++
Personal organization, has good sense of time*	+++	+	+++	+
Integrity, has a well established value system which has been tested in various ways in the past*	+++	++	+	+
Social responsibility, appreciates the need to assume leadership with respect to that responsibility*	+ (?)	+ (?)	+ (?)	–
TOTAL =	40	39	23	27

*Adapted from Harry Levinson, "Criteria for Choosing Chief Executives," 1980.

the degree to which they can work independently, and the degree to which they use a well-tested value system (though the reader may not always agree with the nature of those values). Existential men do not score negatively on a single dimension, and receive a total of 39 points.

Administrative men score very highly on three of Levinson's dimensions. These are the degree to which they see themselves involved as a participating member of the organization, their ability to exhibit a high level of physical and mental stamina and their personal organization. They also score well on their capacity to abstract, conceptualize, and integrate data for decisions, their ability to judge when to act, their sense of vision both about their careers and the development of the organization, and their capacity to persevere. Administrative men, unlike their rational and existential colleagues, receive negative ratings on six dimensions of leadership: their tolerance for ambiguity, their feeling that they belong in positions of leadership, their ability to nurture and sustain healthy relationships with their superiors, their ability to accept appropriate dependency needs, their ability to be adaptable and manage conditions of stress, and their sense of humor. Administrative men receive a leadership score of 17 points.

Using Levinson's criteria we see that entrepreneurial men are better suited for positions of leadership than administrative men, but less well suited than rational or existential men. Entrepreneurs score very highly on those dimensions that measure the degree to which they have feelings of authority and the belief that they belong in the boss's role, their degree of physical as well as mental stamina, and their ability to persevere in the face of setbacks. Entrepreneurial men also score well on their capacity to abstract, conceptualize, and organize data, their tolerance for ambiguity and confusion, the degree to which they can work independently, their ability to be adaptable and capable of handling stress, and their sense of vision. Entrepreneurial men score negatively on five dimensions. These include the degree to which they are oriented toward the organization's success rather than their own personal aggrandizement, their sensitivity toward other people's feelings, their ability to foster and maintain healthy relationships with authority figures and people of power, their sense of humor, and their sense of social responsibility. Summing Levinson's criteria, we see that entrepreneurial men receive a score of 22 points.

Though Levinson's criteria for choosing leaders ignores the motivational bases of the behavior they measure (for example, whether the leader acts out of feelings of inadequacy and for self-validation, or whether he works out of a genuine desire to improve the organization), and though a summed score assumes that all criteria are of equal importance, we are able to conclude that by an independently constructed index of leadership qualities rational and existential men score considerably higher than administrators and entrepreneurs.

We have seen the 20 personal qualities that Levinson feels should be part of the leader's cognitive makeup, and we have seen how our four types match up on each of Levinson's normative criteria. We must now see if the qualities we have attributed to leaders and managers, and those attributed to leaders and managers by other investigators, may be used together to provide a general psychological framework by which the two types of powerholder may be differentiated.

ARE LEADERS AND MANAGERS DIFFERENT?

It became evident in Chapter 6 that not all of our leadership types are actually leaders; that is, not all are people who initiate action and mold the energies and ambitions of other men. More often than not career bureaucrats are "technocrats" or simply managers. They are specialists who are singularly adept at enforcing existing company policy and completing process-oriented tasks. But they are not motivated (or compelled) to take the risks associated with creating norms and transforming existing company policy into exciting strategies for change. Managerial effectiveness and leadership effectiveness are not synonymous.

One colonel who is now involved in teaching courses in military leadership has told this writer that the military tries to inculcate leadership qualities in their officers. Yet they know full well that only a small fraction of their people can ever be "leaders"—most are just (using the colonel's own term) "managers." In a similar vein, several scholars of organizational behavior have commented that the staid managerial role of the classic bureaucrat is functionally determined by the generic properties of large-scale organizations (Parsons, 1964; Merton, 1965). These scholars maintain that in the first instance bureaucracies strongly attract those who achieve productivity and security by immersion in an intricate and exact system of functional responsibilities. And second, that in spite of the particular and unique strengths and weaknesses that characterize organizational power holders, large organizations naturally homogenize people and induce and reward system maintenance. The "leader" is truly extraordinary in that such a person can ignore, or somehow evade, the ever visible norms of his larger social setting and display behavior based on his or her own needs, drives, values, and goals.

Can leaders and managers be differentiated by distinct sets of personality characteristics? This is a difficult question. Social scientists cannot even agree what leadership is!

PUBLISHED EVIDENCE: LEADERS AS COMPOSED OF A DUALITY OF MIND

Studies of leaders number not in the hundreds, but in the thousands. In discussing published research that has sought to uncover the personality dynamics of leaders, it is necessary that we be parsimonious. Stodgill (1974) alone reports the findings of more than 500 authors. Our purpose here is not to provide a comprehensive review of the literature, but to find key commonalities among the personality traits attributed to leaders in a handful of well-known studies. The findings of these works, presented in Table 7.2, cover several situational contexts but (in general) apply to leaders in business organizations or leaders in small work groups.[4]

If studies of powerful leaders have anything in common, it is the shared conclusion that leaders have a strong need to demonstrate their power. Argyris (1959) maintains that leaders are characterized by a quality that he calls "powermindedness." Zalesnik (1977) maintains that leaders are typified by their use of power to influence the thoughts and actions of other people. Borg (1960) maintains that leaders are marked by a preponderance of "aggressive" and assertive qualities that are used to secure nonconformist ends. Mann (1959), after reviewing more than 20 studies of leaders, concluded that the "need for dominance," extroversion, and the display of "masculine" (that is, powerful and controlling) qualities have all been observed among leaders, while Stodgill (1974) found aggressiveness, extroversion, and a need for dominance also to be of critical importance in the cognitive makeup of leaders. Though they did not study powerholders per se, both Winter (1973) and McClelland (1976) conclude that the salient feature of those who seek power is the experience of having impact on others. Power is a social relation.

It is not surprising that the single most recurrent theme in the study of organizational elites is that leaders exhibit aggressive, dominating tendencies and leadership styles. What is surprising, however, is that coupled with the powerladen qualities attributed to leaders is the ubiquitous finding that leaders simultaneously possess strong "self-control" (Randle, 1956; Weber, 1958; Argyris, 1959; Bennis and Schein, 1966; Stodgill, 1974; McClelland, 1976; Mazlish, 1976). On the one hand, scholars portray leaders as fascinated with power and status, preoccupied with shaping the thoughts and actions of others, in need of obtaining satisfaction through the imposition of structure, and predisposed toward domineering and masculine behavior. They delight in taking bold risks, are consumed with creating impact, and experience lively fantasies of power and control. On the other hand, these same scholars have portrayed leaders as highly inhibited and possessed of a strong superego.

While the findings of our own study do not enable us to enumerate a whole range of systematic differences that distinguish leaders from managers, our evidence is highly suggestive. Our two "leaders" (rational and existential men) are initiative takers. Not only are they marked by positive self-regard, extroversion, dominance, persuasiveness, activity (vs. passivity), and other power-oriented qualities but, as it turns out, our leaders are more likely to be promoted in an accelerated fashion, they show a greater concern for symbols of power in unconscious motivation, and they have acquired greater visible power (that is, they have a significantly

Table 7.2: The Leader's Personality: Convergences of Findings in Five Studies

This Study	Randle (1956)	Mann (1959)	Stodgill (1974)	Zalesnik (1977)
Has very high self-esteem			Displays strong self-confidence	
Is extroverted		Is extroverted	Is extroverted	
Displays domineering qualities		Displays a need for dominance	Is domineering	
Has a very high "activity" level				Is active rather than reactive; shapes ideas rather than responds to them
Is inhibited				
Has strong power needs	Has very strong drive	Displays "masculine" characteristics	Shows agressiveness, ambition	Uses power to influence the thoughts and actions of others
Displays moderate achievement needs.			Has a strong need for achievement; displays a desire to do well	
Displays moderate affiliation needs				
Is promoted rapidly	Performs well; achieves objective results; is results oriented			
Acquires greater visible power				

Takes unsolicited
initiatives

Shows initiative; is a
self-starter

Takes initiative and
shows a willingness to
assume responsibility

Creates challenges;
displays other self-
starter behavior

Is highly motivated and
ambitious

Has an "urge" to get
things done; is not
easily discouraged.

Is highly intelligent

Exhibits an ability to
evaluate situations

Develops fresh approaches
to long-standing
problems

Has above-average
intellectual ability;
shows good judgement

Stimulates the ambitions
of associates; displays
"opinion leadership"
qualities

Motivates others and
receives their loyalty
and cooperation

Is stable and possesses
emotional control

Can be either "internal"
or "external" in control

Organizes and displays
control

Is non-conservative in
actions

Displays orginality

Is creative, tries fresh
approaches

Shows interpersonal
sensitivity

Has "social insight";
sympathetic under-
standing

Is well adjusted (vis a vis
group norms)

Shows persistence in the
face of obstacles

Table 7.2 (con.):

Works well in situations
which are ambiguous

face of obstacles

Is highly adaptable

Possesses soundness and
finality of judgement

Has strength of conviction

Seeks independence

Is tolerant of stress

Tempermentally disposed
to seek out risk and
danger, especially where
opportunity and reward
appear high

Pays attention to *what*
events and decisions
mean

greater number of subordinates reporting to them in their present positions) (see Tables 7.3 and 7.4). This visible power is power that may be displayed.[5]

What the present study and most other studies of leaders do not have in common is the finding that leaders are inhibited. Quite the opposite. What has been shown to be of critical importance to rational and existential men is their lack of inhibition. What is crucial for these leaders is their endemic psychological ability to act on their power needs.

If, as nearly all available evidence (with the exception of the present study) indicates, leaders are constructed of the antithetical central tendencies of power and self-control, then indeed their personality conflicts are truly profound. Consider the wrenching anxiety and tension ever present in a person whose essence, whose fundamental impulse is the pursuit and exercise of power, but whose will sublimates and prohibits the acting out of this impulse. If the unfolding of the psychological events that resolve the inner conflict between power and self-control constitutes the central psychological dynamic in the life history of the leader, then this life history can be called nothing less than psychopathological. It is a life history experienced by a Hitler or a Stalin, but it is surely atypical of successful organizational leaders, among whom the conflict between power strivings and self-control was largely resolved or somehow mitigated in childhood and/or young adult experiences.

Among the group of powerholders we have studied either of two developmental sequences occurred (probably during early childhood). Either the superego came forward and subjugated the impulse to act—in which case the seeds of a managerial style were sown—or the impulse to act gained ascendency over the superego and the psychological antecedent of leadership was realized. The omnipresent clash of ego and superego, so characteristic of Freudian dialecticism, is but a rare malady among our organizational elite. What is remarkable is that the resolution of childhood conflict is often felt years later, resulting in the betterment of the organization.

NARCISSISM: A NECESSARY CONCOMITANT TO POWER?

The possession of power (especially that which is compensatory by nature) must be demonstrated in order for it to have psychological meaning for the powerholder. The powerseeker's attraction to uncertain and bold risks has little to do with the specific circumstances surrounding the risk itself, or even the instrumental (corporeal) reward associated with success; it has everything to do with the psychological satisfaction experienced by one who observes others observing his success. It is the social

Table 7.3: Rates of Promotion Among Leaders and Managers*

Group	N	None	One	Two	Total percent of group-members with one or more accelerated promotions
		Accelerated Promotions (%)			
1. Leaders	51	68.6	27.4	3.9	31.4
2. Managers	50	74.0	18.0	8.0	26.0
3. Whole Military Elite[†]	113	72.9	21.3	5.8	27.1

*Promotion rates cover an average of 12 years in the organization.

[†]Except "leaders" and "managers."

$X^2 = 1.80$, NS (Groups 1 and 2).

$X^2 = 1.93$, NS (Groups 1, 2, and 3).

Table 7.4: Number of Subordinates Reporting to Leaders and Managers

Group	N	$\bar{X}$	SD	t	p value
Leaders	63	66.60	41.01		
Managers	62	28.73	35.09	9.01	.001

162

impact of risk taking that is psychologically attractive. It is the inner feeling of potency derived from projecting an aura of boldness and strength that is so important to those who are characterized by the presence of the power motive.

The notion that power is only meaningful if it is exercised suggests that leaders are considerably more narcissistic than managers. Or it may be that leaders are better psychologically equipped to express their narcissism. What is clear is that the actual display of power is (for many leaders) the significant concomitant to the achievement of power—thus the concept of power as currency.

The need to display power is not a mere surface condition nor is it clear that it is always a reaction formation to other deeply held aspects of personality (such as insecurity or self-doubt). The need to display power or make others aware of one's superior status (or actual capabilities if indeed they do exist) is inherent in the leader's character. Not only is it psychologically prepotent, but it is clearly tied to specific forms of activistic behavior.

Gardner Murphy (1966: 492) has said that self-love (and accompanying love of parent) "may be regarded as the core of the problem of personality adjustment." And further, "what passes for aggression may be self-expression, arising from the fact that in most societies *satisfaction with the self comes from power*" (p. 557) (italics supplied). The link between self-gratification and the pursuit of status and power is, for many leaders, a direct one.

We are not implying that the narcissism exhibited by organizational leaders is of such magnitude that it constitutes a personality disorder.[6] We are saying that without the need to mold the thoughts and ambitions of others, there can be no leadership. Leadership, by definition, implies the qualities of directing, guiding, commanding. It implies active rather than reactive behavior. It also implies that there are those who follow, those who are lead, those who are guided, and those who are commanded. According to the principles of the narcissistic personality syndrome, leaders relate implicitly to followers with the hope (and need) that they confirm the grandiose strivings that the leader so badly wants (Etheredge, 1979).

MANAGERS: ACQUIRERS AND USERS OF ANONYMOUS POWER

In contrast to leaders, managers most often come to acquire anonymous power, or power that may be exercised behind the scenes. The manager does not try to impress others with power tactics, for he fears people's dislike, even their disapproval. The comparative analysis of managerial traits presented in Table 7.5 confirms this contention. Managers have been found to be highly dependent upon the opinions and evaluations of others for the satisfaction of deeply held personality needs. The central struggle of managers is not one of freeing a caged impulse to do, but it is one of winning social acceptance. This acceptance is won through adoption of the norms imposed by the managers' larger social unit.

Following the sacrosanct proscriptions of normative behavior is inimical to the leader. Not only is the leader bent on creating impact (thus his use of novel tactics and his attraction to nonconformist ends), but he is confident that he will achieve his goals. Leaders have strong power or control motivations that they are unafraid to express in practical conduct. They are uninhibited people whose need to demonstrate power is not blocked by an imposing superego or a fear of failure. Managers also harbor strong motivations, but these motivations are not acted out.

What appears to be necessary for a desire for power (the precondition for the pursuit and attainment of power) is the element of narcissism: the need to express and *demonstrate* one's potency. In its classical form narcissism does not imply an unnecessary abundance of self-love, but a yearning for self-understanding and self-expression (Edinger, 1972). Murphy (1966) feels that this yearning assumes an unceasing form: "When a person works his way foward against obstacles until he has achieved power . . . he must use it to gain still more." (p. 557). A weak superego allows the leader to act out these strivings (Kohut, 1971: 232).

In the absence of a controlling superego, power strivings are neither conflicted nor subdued. The power personality, then, is composed of these three elements: a psychological need for power, a need to express power once it is obtained, and a weak superego. The result is a highly power motivated leader whose inner qualities do not inhibit the acting out of strongly held personal strivings. Whether the behavior that is driven by such an orientation results in the betterment of the organization is impossible to predict. Some leaders manifest what is known as "idealized transference," and work to improve the institutions to which they belong and from which they derive their identity; others do not, and simply accumulate personal rewards.

LEADERS, MANAGERS, AND LASSWELL'S THEORY OF THE "HOMO POLITICUS"

The development of our four types showed that the nature of organizational leadership is perhaps more complex than our original

Table 7.5: The Managerial Personality: Convergences of Findings in Four Studies

This Study *(The "Administrative Man")*	*Lasswell (1930)* *(The "Administrator")*	*Whyte (1956)* *(The "Organization Man")*	*Zalesnik (1977)* *(The "Manager")*
Shows a very strong need for affiliation; needs the approval of others for self-validation	"... are bound to individuals very closely." "Had an inability to emancipate himself very far from the reactions of people in his immediate environment" (case study of "H", pp. 128 ff)	Displays a very strong urge to belong (this is his most characteristic trait); is preoccupied with group work.	Maintains a low level of emotional involvement in relationships, but prefers to work with people. Solitary activity brings anxiousness.
Displays strong goal orientation, strong need for achievement in unconsious motivation.	"Displays affects upon less generalized objects." "Has originality of plans ... fertility of mind." (case study of "I" pp. 135ff.)		Tends to adopt impersonal, if not passive attitudes towards goals; goals arise out of necessity rather than desires; goals are organizationally determined.
Takes process-oriented initiatives	"Are coordinators of effort in continuing activity".	Is unconcerned with the what or why; *how* interests the manager; shows great interest in techniques.	Pays attention to *how* things get done.
Sociometric evidence (Boyatzis, 1973) shows high need affiliative people are considered egotistical, arrogant.	"Behaves arrogantly toward subordinates." "Offended every man in his company." (case study of "H", pp. 128 ff.)		

165

Table 7.5: Managerial Personality (cont.)

Is highly insecure.	"... feels a strong sense of insecurity, inadequacy." (case study of "H", pp. 128 ff.)	
Displays strong need for approval by others; exhibits strong fear of rejection.	"The most striking thing is his prolonged worry about his adjustment to specific persons." (case study of "H", pp. 128 ff.)	
Shows strong need for encouragement (from superiors residing inside the organization).	"... is strongly dependent (upon his wife) for praise." (case study of "I", pp. 135 ff.)	
Shows a desire to get ahead	Displays "passive ambition".	
Represses strongly held motives; is introverted; has an avoident orientation	Are greatly repressed, feel a sense of guilt	
Experiences a strong feeling of control		Becomes anxious around disorder
Experiences a powerful sense of responsibility.	"... has a powerful thirst for responsibility, a thirst for authority." (case study of "J" pp. 139 ff.)	Very strong personal identification with the organization; holds strong ideals of duty and responsibility.
		Shows little "skepticism toward the system.
Trusts others in the organization, but the trust is	Believes in and trusts the organization.	Uses the organization to validate his sense of self-worth.

based on feelings of power-
lessness, dependency

Dislikes competition.

Uses methods that are always
aggressive (case study of "H"
pp. 135 ff.)

"In situations which involve
(his) fate he is noticeably
overtense." (case study of "H"
pp. 128 ff.)

Engages in total absorption in
work; absorption is self-
imposed.

Engages in rational activity
by which he eliminates choices.

Displays a strong instinct for
survival which moderates his
sense of risk.

Appears flexible in his use of
tactics.

167

theory suggested. Because activism is not a reflex response to personal insecurity, the mere presence or absence of anxiety tells us little about why powerholders behave the way they do.

Anxieties are mediated by a dynamic interaction of world view and self. The nature of the world view (whether it be threatening or altruistic) as well as the nature of the self (whether it be secure or insecure), delineates a range of ways that personal and control-related anxieties will be managed. Anxiety-reduction need not, and often cannot, result in activistic, initiative-taking behavior. Initiative taking does not occur simply as a reaction to an uncontrollable world or the experience of personal insecurity. Nor does it occur solely as a natural manifestation of the "healthy" personality.

At least since the appearance of *Psychopathology and Politics*, social scientists have been trying to figure out what role insecurity does play in the life of the leader. In that work Harold Lasswell offered the following formula to characterize the politically powerful man:

$$p \} d \} r = \text{Political Man}$$

The first component p stands for the private motives of the individual "as they are nurtured and organized in relation to the family constellation and the early self"; the second term, d, describes the displacement of private motives (from family objects) to public objects; and the third symbol, r, signifies the rationalization of the displacement in terms of public interests. For Lasswell, the "homo politicus" harbored strongly held private motives that were displaced onto public objects and then rationalized in the public interest. What was absolutely necessary was the rationalization process, for private motives (such as personal gain) in the absence of rationalization were believed to be secondary.

As brilliant as Lasswell's famous explanation is, we have seen that it suffers from overgeneralization. The famous p } d } r formula should not be invoked as an explanatory device in the analysis of all leaders (or for that matter, as Lasswell suggested, all "political men"). It is only appropriate in the case of those individuals whose vision of the world enables them to sustain a reasonable expectation that their actions will make a difference. Only then will private motives be displaced onto public objects. Threatening world views promote not the displacement, but the repression, of private motives—internalization is the process outcome.

By employing Lasswell's formula and two additional variants, we may be able to draw some important psychodynamic distinctions between leaders and managers. Lasswell's formula and its variants are

1. $p \} d \} r =$ Leaders

2. $p \} R \} r = $ ⎫
3. $p \} R \} i = $ ⎭ Managers

In the first instance private motives are displaced onto public objects and rationalized in the public interest. This displacement process characterizes the activist leader, the man who lives out his fantasies of power and control. It characterizes the man who does not fear the consequences of his actions and who hopes in some way to mold the energies or thoughts of other men.

In the second case, private motives are repressed (or internalized) and only then are they rationalized in the public interest. This process is characteristic of some kinds of managers and, in particular, the "administrative man"—the manager who avoids acting out his fantasies for fear of negative consequences. Here the anticipation of negative outcomes produces the holding back of private motivations. Unlike Lasswell's man, who rationalizes his actions in the public interest, it is the administrator's proclivity for avoidance which is rationalized in the public (or corporate) interest. Says our administrator, "I must control my power strivings for the sake of the organization. I must channel my achievement strivings so that the goals of the organization may be realized. If everyone went around and did as they pleased, there would be not organization . . . only chaos."

Of course, what is happening here is that the administrative man is afraid to act out (or displace) his most strongly held motive dispositions. The manager lacks the courage to fail; but his fear is cloaked in the guise of "self-control," "responsibility," and "duty." All are organizationally accepted traits.

In the third case, private motives are simply repressed. Discomfort, anxiety, and unhappiness flow from the self-imposed repression of important personality needs. Strongly held motives are not acted out or lived— they are continuously frustrated in their search for practical expression. The repressed powerholder bears resemblance to the classic entrepreneur. He is a loner, apart from the organization, and unable to accept the rules and norms imposed by formal structure. Yet his superego exerts an even more powerful influence than Weber suggested. Introjection rather than displacement is the process outcome here.

Figures 7.1 through 7.3 juxtapose Lasswell's $p \} d \} r$ formula and its variants with the personality dynamics of our four leadership types. This

Figure 7.1: The Personality Dynamics of the Leader

	TYPE	SUBTYPE
Character (Private Motive)	LEADER p ⟩ d ⟩ r	Rational Man / Existential Man
	Displaced Onto Public Objects	*Rationalized In the Coporate Interest*
Internal Control or External Control	Acts with Confidence	Takes Initiatives (As a Strategy to Gain Influence)
High Self esteem	Needs to Control	
Moderate N Power or Strong N Power	Closely Supervises Subordinates	"Runs a 'tight ship'" (When Reality Imposes Structure)
	Lives Fantasies of Power	
"Dominance"	Competitive Orientation	"Innovates" (When Maximizing Gains or Imposing Will)
	Displays power tactics	

Extroversion "Activity"

Figure 7.2: The Personality Dynamics of the Manager

Character (Private Motive)	TYPE	p ⟩ R ⟩ r	SUBTYPE	
	MANAGER	Repressed	Administrative Man	Rationalized in the Corporate Interest
Internal Control				
Insecurity		Feels Personal Responsibility		"Responsibility"
Strong N Achievement → Introversion →		Dislikes competition, confrontation		"Self-Control"
Strong N Affiliation		Displays Deference		"Technical Competence"
High Trust		Is Problem-solving minded		"Loyalty"
Moderate/High Inhibition		Is Approval Seeking, Shows conformance		"Duty"

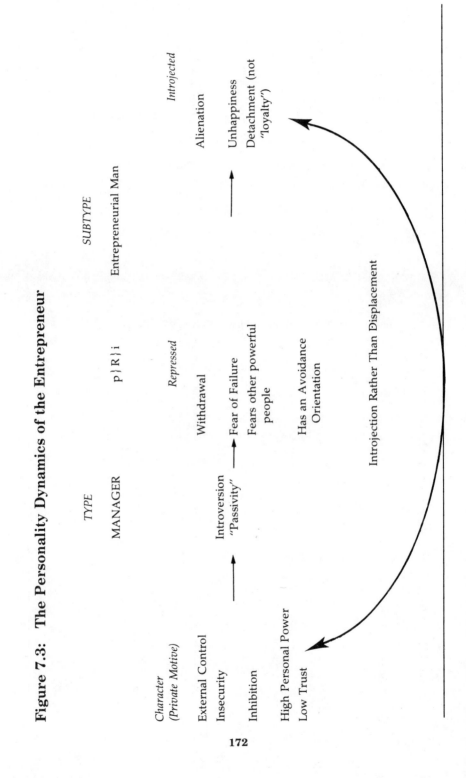

Figure 7.3: The Personality Dynamics of the Entrepreneur

	TYPE		SUBTYPE
	MANAGER	p ⟩ R ⟩ i	Entrepreneurial Man

Character (Private Motive)

		Repressed	*Introjected*
External Control	Introversion "Passivity" →	Withdrawal	Alienation
Insecurity		Fear of Failure	Unhappiness
Inhibition		Fears other powerful people	Detachment (not "loyalty")
High Personal Power		Has an Avoidance Orientation	
Low Trust			

Introjection Rather Than Displacement

juxtaposition enables us to distinguish leaders from managers. Evidence presented throughout this work and in Figure 7.1 suggests that rational and existential men act much as Lasswell's formula would predict. They harbor strong private motives that they displace onto public objects. Their behavior is then rationalized in the corporate interest. The existential man seeks the control of others, frequently takes initiatives, and is not at all fearful of competition, confrontation, or the potentially negative consequences of his actions. Both the rational and existential men approach life's challenges rather than avoid them. They are not dependent upon others for personal satisfaction or the formulation of their goals; their motivations are intrinsic, their achievements emanating from sheer force of will. They believe that their actions can make a difference and they have the courage to fail.

Our administrative man represses rather than displaces his private motives (see Figure 7.2). He then rationalizes them in the corporate (and not coincidentally his own) interest. The critical psychological activity here is the repression of personal motivations and ambitions. The repressed powerholder seeks not the control of others but their approval. The motivations of administrative man are thus extrinsically defined and hidden beneath a veneer he understands as the "public interest." He is "responsible," "technically competent," "loyal," "dutiful," and most importantly, he is needed by the organization.

The entrepreneur also represses his private motives but does not (or cannot) rationalize them in the public interest, for they never become displaced (see Figure 7.3). He fears and mistrusts powerful people and actually withdraws from social intercourse. His behavior is avoident, even escapist. He is unconcerned with or unable to focus in on the corporate interest. The ultimate entrepreneurial act is the breaking away from the organization and the acceptance of the risk associated with the formation of the new enterprise.

THE ROLE OF WILL

Initiative taking may occur either as a reaction to an irrational or a rational world, only when the initiative taker retains a strong belief that it is at least possible that his actions will make a difference. People who believe that their actions matter may be secure or insecure, but they are somehow able to project, or displace, or externalize their anxieties. In Lasswell's words, they are able to work out their private anxieties by displacing them onto public objects. Without a sense of hope, immured in despair, a rational and logical world will do little to promote action. Just because a world is understandable does not mean it is changeable or worth changing.

The leader who lacks the elements of hope and will represses, sublimates, or otherwise manages his anxieties and insecurities through the process of internalization. This type of leader is really not a leader at all. He may be an "administrator" or even a "theorist," but he is likely to be a manager—he is not a leader of men.

The extent to which initiatives will be taken is the result of the interface between the way one feels about oneself and the way in which one views the world. A combinatorial pattern that permits externalization is characteristic of the leader who attempts to transform systems; the interface of world view and self that promotes internalization is characteristic of the manager who feels most secure promoting the status quo.

CONCLUSION: PERSONALITY AND LEADERSHIP

The use of reason and analytic behavior displayed by rational men, the use of power tactics and the bold initiative-taking style of existential men, the deferential need for approval and the achieving behavior exhibited by administrative men, and the mistrustful, emotional style which marks entrepreneurial men all have their roots in type-specific, unique, and complex internal states of mind. These unique configurations of personality make leaders and managers who and what they are by creating differing world views which in turn function as qualitatively dissimilar interpretive frameworks by which the organization and its problems are perceived and understood.

Existential men are not only skeptical of their ability to control but they are also extroverted, uninhibited, self-confident and in need of power. Administrative men are not only insecure and in need of positive evaluation by others, but they also believe strongly in personal causation and display a consuming need to achieve. Leaders and managers are not only power-seekers, or self-confident, or in need of nurturance, or extroverted, or anxiety-ridden. They are all of these and much more, but in varying degrees. Leadership style is never singularly determined. It is the product of multiple causative factors and oftentimes countervailing and paradoxical psychological forces. In order to understand leadership behavior, we must understand the pull and push of the forces which underlie that behavior—we must understand the essence of the man in the leader.

NOTES

1. About the socialization processes that shape the personalities of political men, Lasswell (1930: 174) states, "There is a deep meaning in the phrase of Paley's that a 'family contains the rudiments of an empire.' The family experience organizes very powerful drives

in successive levels of integration, and these primitive attitudes are often called into play as the unobserved partners of social relations."

2. Those studies that have recognized the complexity and variability of the ways in which personality and social context act in concert to impinge upon, or drive behavior, are somehow more difficult to remember than those that boldly state that behavior is singularly determined. Those studies (for example, Smith, 1968) that offer changing conditions under which certain factors are likely to surface and/or predominate are not as neat and tidy as we (in our natural efforts to simplify, to break down) would wish. The images they evoke, are therefore less vivid. Yet as accurate descriptors of reality they do justice to social science.

3. For example, in judging administrative men we have attributed to them characteristics found by McClelland and other researchers to be part of the high need achiever's personal makeup.

4. The author has purposefully avoided discussion of biographical studies of leaders. Not only do the methodologic underpinnings of such works differ radically from those of the present study, but their sheer number make any comparative synthesis a logistic impossibility.

5. The percent difference in the rates of promotion among leaders and managers is not dramatic or statistically significant. It may well be that the people we have classified as leaders come to acquire greater visible positions of command when they do get promoted, though their rates of promotion are only slightly more accelerated than nonleaders. In any case, the reader should remember that these rates of promotion do not include the business sample (for which such data were unavailable), and that leaders in military organizations who employ strong, sometimes novel strategies of style will not always be rewarded (or appreciated) for their actions. A more adequate test of our tacit assumption that "leaders" will rise more rapidly than "managers" would have to make use of comparative data on the promotion rates of our business executives.

6. The key internal feature of the narcissistic personality disorder is the simultaneous existence in the mind of two different and unintegrated subjective experiences of the self (Etheredge, 1979). In the foreground of the mind is the element of insecurity and deeply rooted self-doubt, but in the background and above, there exists the "grandiose self"—that part of the person that leads him or her to believe he or she can accomplish anything (Kohut, 1971). This grandiose sector of the mind is highly charged and pervades the professional life of the leader (Etheredge, 1979). Among men, the origin of this disorder has been said to be the circumstances that surround growing up under the wing of a very powerful and domineering mother (Friedlander and Cohen, 1975).

APPENDIXES

OPERATIONAL DEFINITIONS
OF THE FOUR LEADERSHIP TYPES

The following procedures were used to formally categorize the four leadership types:

First, both business and military populations were merged into one Statistical Package for the Social Sciences (SPSS) file. Next, two histograms or scatterplots were produced to provide the author with the full frequency distributions of the two primary typology variables, self-esteem/insecurity and locus of control.* In order to provide "maximum discrepancy" or "pull" from the dependent variables of the study, the author then selected out those business and military elites who satisfied the following criteria. (Note: As indicated in Chapter 1, the self-esteem index had a normalized range of between 0 and 100; the range of the locus of control index was between 0 and 21, with six items being "fillers.")

Rational Man: Self-esteem index is greater than or equal to 79 and less than or equal to 95 *and* locus of control index is greater than or equal to 1 and less than or equal to 6.

Existential Man: Self-esteem index is greater than or equal to 79 and less than or equal to 95 *and* locus of control index is greater than or equal to 10 and less than or equal to 21.

Administrative Man: Self-esteem index is greater than or equal to 38 and less than or equal to 68 *and* locus of control index is greater than or equal to 10 and less than or equal to 21.

Entrepreneurial Man: Self-esteem index is greater than or equal to 38 and less than or equal to 68 *and* locus of control index is greater than or equal to 10 and less than or equal to 6.

---

*These variables are not dichotomous but continuous.

These criteria were selected after breaking both the self-esteem and locus of control distributions into thirds.* Thus our four types take in a subsample of 133 men. Figure A.1 is a graphic representation of the operationalized types.

---

*Selecting the top and bottom quartiles would have produced more intertype variance (that is, more dramatic differences between types), but the idea of using that criterion was abandoned because such a selection process would have seriously reduced the number of subjects to be placed into each quadrant of the typology.

Figure A.1: Operationalization of the Four Types

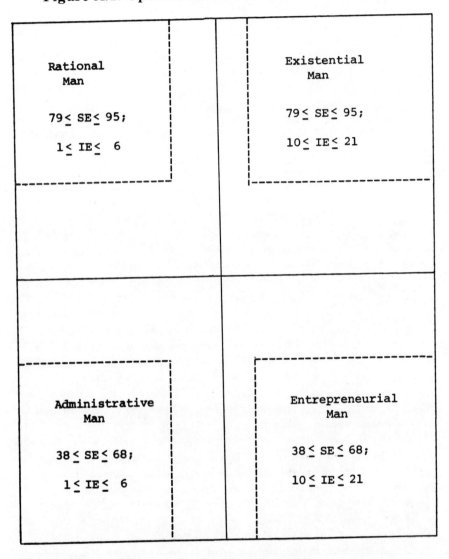

Rational
Man

$79 \leq SE \leq 95;$

$1 \leq IE \leq 6$

Existential
Man

$79 \leq SE \leq 95;$

$10 \leq IE \leq 21$

Administrative
Man

$38 \leq SE \leq 68;$

$1 \leq IE \leq 6$

Entrepreneurial
Man

$38 \leq SE \leq 68;$

$10 \leq IE \leq 21$

A NOTE ON SCORING OF THE FATE-CONTROL CONSTRUCT

The locus of control measure (also referred to as "I-E") employed in the questionnaire is the original 29-item scale devised by Julian Rotter (1966). Respondents theoretically score between 0 and 23, with one point being given for every "external" response. Six questions (or scale items) are "fillers" having no locus of control value. "Internality-externality" is a relative measure, with a high score indicating a perceived external locus of control, and a low score, a perceived internal locus of control.

As the I-E construct has recently been factor-analyzed (Mirels, 1970; Reid and Ware, 1973) and seen to be of a multidimensional nature, we present whole locus scores and its decomposed separable factors. Belief in control with regard to the self will be referred to as "personal control" (or Factor I), and belief in control with regard to the environment will be called "system control" (or Factor II).

Belief in the ability to control one's actions need not be related to one's belief in the ability to control one's environment. For example, many of the business executives in this study believed strongly in their sense of personal control, yet doubted their ability to influence more remote "extrinsic" forces (such as "the economy"), which inevitably affect their decisions. Personal and system control can, of course, have interactive effects, yet they need not be intimately related or vary concomitantly.

Although the great majority of studies employing the IE measure do show internals to be more goal-directed and instrumental, at least three studies (Gurin et al., 1969; Forward and Williams, 1970; Lao, 1970) have shown that externals participate in system-changing modes of behavior. A substantial number of business and military elites are relatively external in their perceived locus of control.

Since most of the literature dealing with the I-E construct utilizes nonelite populations (that is, children, students, and minorities), the potential compatibility of an external orientation and formal positions of power and status has not been previously tested. Instead, an inferential error has pervaded thinking on this subject (Rothberg, 1980). Because powerless groups have been found to be on the whole relatively external, it has been reasoned, and erroneously so, that powerful groups must be internal. Such is clearly not the case. While the average locus score of the business and military elite who participated in this study is quite close to the average locus score of the typical college student, a large intra-elite variance exists. As illustrated through the presentation of nonelite baseline data, a significant number of powerful elite individuals do not believe they are in complete control of their fate. While the sense of externality does not limit the attainment of formal positions of power and influence (and in fact may actually enhance it), it strongly affects the expression of power.

In the following table, the whole I-E construct is broken down into the two separable dimensions used in this study. The breakdown is based on the Reid and Ware factor analysis. I-E numbers correspond to items presented in Robinson and Shaver (1973).

FACTOR I	FACTOR II
Personal Control	*System Control*
I-E2, I-E4, I-E6, I-E10, I-E12	I-E3, I-E9, I-E16, I-E21, I-E28
I-E14, I-E15, I-E17, I-E19, I-E20	
I-E23, I-E27, I-E29	

A NOTE ON SCORING OF THE TAT PROTOCOL

Each of the three TAT pictures used in this study was selected in consultation with a professional testing service (McBur and Company). The pictures have been widely used with a variety of occupational groups and have been tested for reliability and validity. Interscorer reliability levels are approximately .87.[1] Each of the pictures was presented to study participants in a randomized sequence. Respondents were asked to describe what they thought was occurring in the pictures. No time limit was imposed for completion of stories.

McBur and Company scored all stories written in response to each picture for need achievement, need power, and need affiliation. If power imagery was present, the story (or stories) was further scored for the four power components: fear of power, hope of power, socialized power, and personalized power.[2] The author scored all pictures for activity inhibition using the McClelland (1976) scoring system. Picture-specific norms are available from the author.

Data presented in the book are uncorrected for word length. There is evidence that the length of stories written is associated with the presence of motive dispositions scored (David Winter, personal communication). The advantage of word-length correction is that data may theoretically be compared across studies employing identical pictures. Unfortunately, however, because of differing test conditions and protocols such comparisons are tenuous. (In addition, interstudy comparisons would only be possible if all stories were corrected for word length by use of the same statistical correction procedures. These procedures are not readily available in published form.) I decided, therefore, that presentation of corrected scores would be of little benefit. Uncorrected scores are easier for the reader to interpret.

NOTES

1. When it was recommended that the "Ship's Captain" picture be used I expressed concern about the possibility of military officers being especially apt to elicit certain types of unconscious motivation as a result of the picture's uniformed character. I was assured that the picture had been tested with at least one sample of military personnel and that scored stories written in response to the Ship's Captain picture did not differ significantly from stories written in response to other TAT pictures.

2. The interested reader may consult *Motivation Workshops* (McClelland and Steele, 1972) for TAT scoring instructions.

Table A.1: A Content Analysis of Stories Written in Response to a Three-Picture TAT Protocol
(Numbers indicate the percent of stories in which categorized incidents occur)

	Story Outcome				Uncertainty	Hierarchic Relations	Hostility	Confidence	Insecurity
	+	−	Neutral	N.O.G.°					
Rational Man	41.2	4.5	27.5	15.5	8.2	11.0	11.0	9.1	4.5
Existential Man	41.8	10.9	34.5	5.4	20.0	23.6	36.3	10.9	9.1
Administrative Man	41.3	13.0	39.1	6.5	8.6	13.0	15.2	13.0	6.1
Entrepreneurial Man	32.7	12.2	30.6	17.3	19.3	16.3	20.4	4.1	6.5

*No outcome given.

186

A COMPARATIVE ANALYSIS OF THE PERSONALITY CHARACTERISTICS OF THE BUSINESS AND MILITARY ELITE

At least one very important objection could be raised concerning the methodological procedures employed in drawing our four leadership types from a combined sample of business and military professionals. The objection is that on the face of it, the kinds of people attracted to corporate and military life are very different. Their personality and motivational characteristics are different; therefore it does not make sense to combine the two groups into one.

Aside from the gross matching procedures employed by the author in selecting parent populations (such as matching for age, religion, sex, and years in the organizational work force), here we report the findings of a more formal comparison of the major personality characteristics of the two groups.

Evidence reported in Table A.2 indicates that aside from the gross demographic commonalities of the two groups, they are also well matched on basic personality characteristics. The objection that the two groups should not be merged into one because of generic characterológical difference is not well-founded.[1]

NOTE

1. The author also tested for differences in birth-order effects for the two groups (as well as for the leadership types). No outstanding differences were found, though the military population does have a slightly higher than expected percentage of firstborn.

Table A.2: A Comparative Analysis of the Personality Characteristics of the Business and Military Populations

	Business		Military	
Characteristic	N	X	N	X·
Self-esteem	70	71.94 (SD = 10.67)	258	73.35 (SD = 9.98)
Locus of Control	66	8.29 (SD = 3.57)	233	8.28 (SD = 3.86)
Factor I	67	2.60 (SD = 1.40)	240	2.20 (SD = 1.60)
Factor II	68	0.53 (SD = 0.70)	242	0.39 (SD = 0.61)
Need Achievement	58	1.87 (SD = 4.79)	211	3.86* (SD = 4.42)
Need Affiliation	58	3.26 (SD = 2.21)	207	3.16 (SD = 1.96)
Need Power	58	3.51 (SD = 3.98)	205	2.84 (SD = 3.40)
Hope for Power	58	1.38 (SD = 1.64)	205	1.27 (SD = 1.80)
Fear of Power	58	0.41 (SD = 1.18)	205	0.60 (SD = 1.33)
Personal Power	58	0.31 (SD = 0.57)	205	0.44 (SD = 0.73)
Social Power	58	0.41 (SD = 0.68)	205	0.47 (SD = 0.88)
Inhibition	57	1.37 (SD = 2.70)	210	1.10 (SD = 1.80)
Activity-Passivity	71	1.91 (SD = 0.75)	261	2.01 (SD = 0.75)
Interpersonal Trust	71	65.30 (SD = 12.35)	258	62.90* (SD = 9.32)
Persuasibility	71	3.04 (SD = 1.14)	260	2.87 (SD = 1.14)
Introversion-Extroversion	71	2.57 (SD = 0.82)	261	2.57 (SD = 0.92)
Dominance	71	3.03 (SD = 0.45)	261	3.07 (SD = 1.06)

*p. < .01 (two-tailed t test).

THE QUESTIONNAIRE

---

*The order of items appearing beyond question 12 was systematically randomized for all participants. All scales contain reversals for possible response set bias.

†In addition the questionnaire included all 29 items of Rotter's (1966) locus of control scale. The scale has not been reproduced here as part of the questionnaire because of its availability elsewhere (see Robinson and Shaver, 1973).

1. Your age is _____

2. Your religion is _____

3. You are attending... Air War College _____
   Air Command and Staff College _____

4. The number of subordinates you supervised in your last
   assignment was _____

5. Your rank is _____

6. Are you rated?----- Yes, a pilot _____ Yes, a navigator _____
   No _____

7. Have you ever been promoted "below the zone?"
   ____Yes, one time   ____Yes, twice; two successive ranks
   ____Yes, twice; but not two successive ranks
   ____Yes, three times   ____No

8. What level of education had you achieved before you entered
   your current P.M.E. school? _____

9. The educational level of your father was? _____

10. The educational level of your mother was? _____

11. Your father's occupation _____

12. Please rank by age, yourself and any brothers and sisters in
    your family (please list youngest first)
    1. _____   3. _____   5. _____
    2. _____   4. _____   6. _____

13. I am...
    Extroverted/----/----/----/----/----/Introverted

14. When trying to tackle a new and difficult job, I often
    need encouragement from (please rank order)
    ____Superiors
    ____Friends and those I love
    ____Work peers
    Other _____

190

15. To what extent do you believe your life's goals are truly your own, and how much are the result of others' expectations?
Completely my own ____   Very much my own ____   Largely my own ____
Not so much my own ____   Not at all my own ____

16. I am...
Active/----/----/----/----/----/Passive

17. Would you consider yourself a person who actively looks for challenges, or someone who becomes motivated primarily through challenges that appear on your desk?
____ I actively look for challenges
____ I become motivated by challenges that appear on my desk

18. I am...   Dominant/----/----/----/----/----/Firm
Encouraging/----/----/----/----/----/Persuasive

19. I believe... My I.Q. is
Far above average/----/----/----/----/----/Somewhat above average

20. It is a popular notion that in order to achieve success in an organization one must conform to the expectations of others. Is this conformity only necessary at lower levels, to end when higher positions are reached, or will conformity always be a necessity?
____ A phase to end; top management can be creative and self-expressive
____ Always a necessity   Other _____

21. How often are you overburdened by work you don't enjoy?
All the time ____   Very often ____   Often ____   Not very often ____   Not at all ____

22. Are you satisfied with the amount of challenges presented you by your work environment?   Completely satisfied ____
Very satisfied ____   Satisfied ____   Not very satisfied ____
Not satisfied at all ____

23(a)* How often do subordinates try to be helpful, and how often do they mostly just look out for themselves? They try to be helpful... All the time ____
Very often ____   Often ____   Not very often ____   Infrequently ____
Not at all ____

---

*The trust scale used in this study included questions 23a through 26b and 63. The formula used was as follows:

Trust = (15 X (5 - Question 63) + 12 X (6 - Question 24a) + 12 X (Question 24b - 1) + 12 X (Question 25a - 1) + 12 X (6 - Question 25b) + 12 X (Question 26a - 1) + 12 X (6 - Question 26b) + 12 X (6 - Question 23a) + 12 X (Question 23b - 1))/5.4

23(b) They mostly look out for themselves...
All the time ____ Very often ____ Often ____ Not very
often ____ Very infrequently ____ Not at all ____

24(a) How often do superiors try to be helpful, and how often do they
just look out for themselves?
They try to be helpful... All the time ____ Very often ____
Often ____ Not very often ____ Infrequently ____
Not at all ____

24(b) They mostly look out for themselves... All the time ____
Very often ____ Often ____ Not very often ____
Infrequently ____ Not at all ____

25(a) How often do you think that most subordinates would try to take
advantage of you if they got the chance, and how often would they
try to be fair?
Try to take advantage... All the time ____ Very often ____
Often ____ Not very often ____ Infrequently ____ Never ____

25(b) Try to be fair... All the time ____ Very often ____
Often ____ Not very often ____ Infrequently ____ Never ____

26(a) How often do you think that most superiors would try to take advantage
of you if they got the chance, and how often would they try to be fair?
Try to take advantage... All the time ____ Very often ____
Often ____ Not very often ____ Infrequently ____ Not at all ____

26(b) Try to be fair... All the time ____ Very often ____ Often ____
Not very often ____ Infrequently ____ Not at all ____

27. Have you tried to convince anyone of your political ideas lately?
____ Yes ____ No

28. Has anyone asked your advice on a political question recently?
____ Yes ____ No

29.* When you have to talk in front of a class or a group of people your own
age, how afraid or worried do you usually feel? Usually very worried ____
Worried ____ Slightly worried ____ Not worried at all ____

30. To what do you attribute your occupational success? (Please rank order:
1 = highest)
____ Peer support   ____ Connections
____ Hard work   ____ Self-confidence
____ A few lucky breaks ____ Family encouragement
____ Being in "the right place at the right time"

---

*The self-esteem scale used in this study included questions 29-34, 38 and 62.
The formula used for the scale was as follows:

$$\text{Self-esteem} = (6 \times (6 - \text{Question } 62) + 10 \times (\text{Question } 29 - 1) + 5 \times (7 - \text{Question } 30) + 6 \times (6 - \text{Question } 31) + 6 \times (6 - \text{Question } 32) + 6 \times (\text{Question } 33 - 1) + 6 \times (6 - \text{Question } 33) + 6 \times (6 - \text{Question } 38))/2.40$$

31. Do you ever feel so discouraged with yourself that you wonder whether anything is worthwhile? Always _____ Very often _____ Often _____ Not very often _____ Very infrequently _____ Never _____

32. When you are required to direct the activities of others, how often do you feel that you receive personal respect from those directed? Always _____ Very often _____ Often _____ Sometimes _____ Rarely _____ Never _____

33. How often do you have the feeling that you can do everything well? Always _____ Very often _____ Often _____ Not very often _____ Very infrequently _____ Never _____

34. How often do you feel you are a successful person? Always _____ Very often _____ Often _____ Not very often _____ Very infrequently _____ Never _____

35. How much do you <u>enjoy</u> yourself on a typical work day? Very much _____ Much _____ Not so much _____ Not at all _____

36. It is only when a person devotes himself to an ideal or a cause that his life becomes meaningful... Strongly agree _____ Agree _____ Slightly agree _____ Slightly disagree _____ Disagree _____ Strongly disagree _____

37. How often do you present superiors with unsolicited recommendations, suggestions? Always _____ Very often _____ Often _____ Not very often _____ Almost never _____

38. When you do present superiors with unsolicited recommendations, usually how certain are you that these recommendations will be acted upon? Usually very certain_____ Usually certain _____ Somewhat certain _____ Somewhat uncertain _____ Uncertain _____ Very uncertain _____

39. It is the duty of each person to do his job the very best he can... Strongly agree _____ Agree _____ Slightly agree _____ Disagree_____ Strongly disagree _____

40. Good leaders are born and not made... Strongly agree _____ Agree _____ Slightly agree _____ Slightly disagree _____ Disagree _____ Strongly disagree _____

41. In which of the following high school or college varsity sports did you participate? _____ Baseball _____ Basketball _____ Crew _____ Football _____Golf _____Gymnastics _____ Hockey _____ Lacrosse _____ Tennis _____Other

42. If as a young man you had inherited a great fortune, would you have pursued your present career? Yes _____ No _____ If not, what would you have done? _____ _____

43. About how often do you actively go out and seek challenges (in the course of your work)? Always ____ Very often ____ Often ____ Not very often ____ Infrequently ____ Not at all ____

44. An ambitious person... (please check the most appropriate)
    ____ Is admired
    ____ Creates enemies
    ____ Both

45. If it became apparent that you could not move into a higher position in your sponsoring organization, would you remain content with your present job?
    ____ Yes ____ No Other _____

46. I have the will to lead other men... ____ Yes ____ No

47. I enjoy competition...
    Very much ____ Much ____ Not so much ____ Not at all ____

48. After attaining a long sought-after goal... please describe your thoughts and feelings
    I _____
    _____
    _____

49. I enjoy new challenges because... (please rank order)
    ____ I enjoy working on a challenging problem for its own sake
    ____ I enjoy the prestige of being given tough challenges that others might shy away from
    ____ The successful accomplishment of the challenge gives me great pleasure

50. Have you ever taken, or thought of taking any of the following self-provement programs? Biofeedback, speedreading, psychoanalysis, Silva mind-control, transcendental meditation. Yes ____ No____

51. It is very often hard for many people to go on with their work if they are not encouraged. How often do you feel you need encouragement? Always ____ Very often ____ Often ____ Sometimes ____ Rarely ____ Never ____

52. In your spare time, do you prefer to relax (by reading, watching T.V., etc) or participate in some activity (jogging, card playing, etc.)?
    ____ I prefer to relax
    ____ I like to participate in some activity

53. How comfortable do you feel in making decisions about which there exist no organizational precedents, groundrules?
    Very uncomfortable ____ Uncomfortable ____
    Slightly uncomfortable ____ Not uncomfortable at all ____

54. Americans today are preoccupied with "finding meaning" in their lives and in their jobs. How often do you find your work personally meaningful, and how

often just a duty? Personally meaningful... Always ____
Most of the time ____ Sometimes ____ Not very often ____ Never ____
Just a duty... Always ____ Most of the time ____ Sometimes ____
Not very often ____ Never ____

55. After successfully completing a long and arduous task, it is very important
to me that people recognize me for my accomplishments... Strongly agree ____
Agree ___ Slightly agree ____ Disagree ____ Strongly disagree ____

56. Upon entering a profession, many people have an idea of what it is they
would like to become. Other people do not, and just make the most of
opportunities that come. When you entered your profession did you have
an idea, a picture of what position, rank you wanted to attain?
    A clear idea/picture ____
    An idea/picture, though unclear ____
    No picture or idea ____
              Has this position been attained? Yes ____ No ____
              Has this position been surpassed? Yes ____ No ____

57. Some people have said that it is possible to be TOO ambitious. Do you
agree? Strongly agree ____ Agree ____ Slightly agree ____ Disagree ____
Strongly disagree ____

58. I try to stimulate the ambition of my associates ...
Very often ____ Often ____ Infrequently ____ Very infrequently ____
Never ____

59. Have you ever run for any public office, or office in a club, fraternity,
student association, etc.?
              Public Office... Yes ____ No ____
              Other office (s) ... Yes ____ No ____

60. Please place an "X" by the word which best describes your political beliefs...
              ____ Extreme liberal
              ____ Liberal
              ____ Moderate liberal
              ____ Extreme conservative
              ____ Conservative
              ____ Moderate conservative
                   -Other _____
              BUSINESS ONLY

61.
    If as a young man you had inherited a great fortune, would you have
    pursued your present career?
         ____ Yes   ____ No
                         If no, what would you have done?
    _____
    _____
    _____

62. How certain are you of your ability to accomplish the tasks which will be re-
    quired of you in the job role(s) for which you are now training?
Very Certain____ Certain____ Slightly Certain____ Slightly Uncertain____
Strongly Uncertain____

63. Generally speaking, how often would you say subordinates can be trusted?
    Allof the time____ Most of the time____ Some of the time____
    Infrequently____ Never____

BIBLIOGRAPHY

Andreski, S. (1968). Method and Substantive Theory in Max Weber. In Eisenstadt, S. N. (Ed.). *The Protestant Ethic and Modernization*. New York: Basic Books, pp. 46–63.

Argyris, C. (1959). *Personality and Organization: The Conflict Between System and the Individual*. New York: Harper & Row.

———. (1960). *Interpersonal Competence and Organizational Effectiveness*. Homewood, Ill.: Dorsey Press.

Aron, R. (1960). Evidence and Inference in History. In Lerner, D. (Ed.). *Evidence and Inference*. Chicago: Free Press.

Atkinson, J. W., and Hoselitz, B. F. (1958). Entrepreneurship and personality. *Explorations in Entrepreneurial History, 10,* 107–112.

Atkinson, J. W., Heyns, R. W., and Veroff, J. (1954). The effect of experimental arousal of the affiliation motive on thematic apperception. *Journal of Abnormal and Social Psychology, 49,* 405–410.

Bakke, E. W. (1955). *The Fusion Process*. New Haven, Conn.: Yale University Press.

Barber, J. D. (1965). *The Lawmakers*. New Haven, Conn: Yale University Press.

Barber, J. D. (1972). *Presidential Character*. New York: Prentice-Hall.

Barnard, C. I. (1938). *The Functions of the Executive*. Cambridge, Mass.: Harvard University Press.

Bartolomé, F. (1972). Executives as human beings. *Harvard Business Review, 50,* 60–70.

Bennis, W. G., and Schein, E. H. (1966). *Douglas McGregor: Leadership and Motivation.* Cambridge, Mass.: MIT Press.

Bills, R., et al. (1951). An index of adjustment and values. *Journal of Consulting Psychology, 15,* 257–261.

Blalock, H. M., Jr. (1972). *Social Statistics.* New York: McGraw-Hill.

Blau, P. M. (1974). *On the Nature of Organizations.* New York: Wiley.

Borg, W. R. (1960). Prediction of small group role behavior from personality variables. *Journal of Abnormal and Social Psychology, 60,* 112–116.

Bottomore, T. B. (1964). *Elites and Society.* Middlesex, England: Pelican Books.

Boyatzis, R. E. (1973). Affiliation Motivation. In McClelland, D. C., and Steele, R. S. (Eds.). *Human Motivation: A Book of Readings.* Morristown, N.J.: General Learning Press.

Byrne, D. (1961). The repression-sensitization scale: rationale, reliability, and validity. *Journal of Personality, 29,* 334–349.

Camus, A. (1955). *The Myth of Sisyphus.* New York: Random House.

Coleman, J. S., et al. (1966). *Equality of Educational Opportunity.* Washington, D.C.: U.S. Government Printing Office.

Collins, O. F., Moore, D. G., and Unwalla, B. D. (1964). *The Enterprising Man.* East Lansing, Mich.: Michigan State University Business Studies.

Cooley, C. H. (1956). *Human Nature and the Social Order.* New York: Free Press.

Crandell, R. (1973). The Measurement of Self-Esteem and Related Constructs. In Robinson, J. P., and Shaver, P. R. (Eds.). *Measures of Social Psychological Attitudes.* Ann Arbor, Mich.: Institute for Social Research.

Crockett, H. C. (1973). The Achievement Motive and Differential occupational Mobility in the United States. In McClelland, D. C., and Steele, R. S. (Eds.). *Human Motivation: A Book of Readings.* Morristown, N.J.: General Learning Press.

Davis, W. L., and Phares, E. J. (1969). Parental antecedents of internal-external control of reinforcement. *Psychological Reports, 24,* 427–36.

De Charms, R. (1968). *Personal Causation.* New York: Academic Press.

Downs, A. (1967). *Inside Bureaucracy.* New York: Free Press.

Edinger, E. G. (1972). *Ego and Archetype.* New York: Putnam's.

Eisenstadt, S. N. (1968). The Protestant Ethic Thesis in an Analytical and Historical Perspective. In Eisenstadt, S. N. (Ed.). *The Protestant Ethic and Modernization.* New York: Basic Books.

Erikson, E. (1973). *Childhood and Society.* Middlesex, England: Penguin Books.

Etheredge, L. S. (1979). Hardball politics: a model. *Political Psychology, 1,* 3–26.

Etzioni, A. (1975). *A Comparative Analysis of Complex Organizations.* New York: Free Press.

Fineman, S. (1977). The achievement motive construct and its measurement: where are we now? *British Journal of Psychology, 68,* 1–22.

Fish, B., and Karabenick, S. (1971). Relationship between self-esteem and locus of control. *Psychological Reports, 29,* 784.

Forward, J. R., and Williams, J. (1970). Internal-external control and black militancy. *Journal of Social Issues, 20,* 72–90.

Friedrich, C. (1950). *The New Image of the Common Man.* Boston: Beacon Press.

Friedlander, S., and Cohen, R. (1975). The personality correlates of billigerence in international conflict. *Comparative Politics, 7,* 155–186.

Greenstein, F. I. (1975). *Personality and Politics: Problems of Evidence, Inference and Conceptualization.* New York: Norton.

Gurin, P., et al. (1969). Internal-external control and the motivational dynamics of Negro youth. *Journal of Social Issues, 25,* 29–53.

Hagen, E. (1962). *A Theory of Social Change.* Homewood, Ill.: Dorsey Press.

Hamilton, R. (1971). A comparative study of five methods of assessing self-esteem, dominance and dogmatism. *Educational and Psychological Measurement, 51,* 441–452.

Hanna, T. (1967). Albert Camus: Man in Revolt. In Schrader, B. A. (Ed.). *Existential Philosophers: Kierkegaard to Merleau-Ponty.* New York: McGraw-Hill.

Harvey, J. M. (1971). Locus of control shift in administrators. *Perceptual and Motor Skills, 33*, 980–982.

Heider, F. (1958). *The Psychology of Interpersonal Relations*. New York: Wiley.

Henry, W. E. (1949). The business executive: the psychodynamics of a social role. *American Journal of Sociology, 54*, 286–291.

Hersch, P. D., and Scheibe, K. E. (1967). On the reliability and validity of internal-external control as a personality dimension. *Journal of Consulting Psychology, 31*, 609–614.

Horney, K. 91939). *New Ways in Psychoanalysis*. New York: Norton.

Hountras, P. T., and Scharf, M. C. (1970). Manifest anxiety and locus of control of low achieving college males. *Journal of Psychology, 74*, 95–100.

Hovland, C. I., Janis, I., and Kelley, H. H. (1953). *Communication and Persuasion*. New Haven, Conn.: Yale University Press.

Hovland, C. I., and Janis, I. (1959). *Personality and Persuasibility*. New Haven, Conn.: Yale University Press.

Hyman, H. H. (1959). *Political Socialization*. New York: Free Press.

Janowitz, M. (1960). *The Professional Soldier*. New York: Free Press.

Joe, V. C. (1971). Review of the internal-external control construct as a personality variable. *Psychological Reports, 28*, 619–640.

Kahn, M. (1969). *Class and Conformity*. Homewood, Ill.: Dorsey Press.

Katz, D., and Kahn, R. (1966). *The Social-Psychology of Organizations*. New York: Wiley.

Katz, D. (1969). The Motivational Basis of Organizational Behavior. In Borgatta, E. (Ed.). *Social-Psychology: Readings and Perspective*. Chicago: Rand McNally.

Kohut, H. (1971). *The Analysis of the Self: A Systematic Approach to the Psychoanalytic Treatment of Narcissistic Personality Disorders*. Monograph Series of the Psychoanalytic Study of the Child. New York: International Universities Press.

Lane, R. E. (1967). *Political Ideology*. New York: Free Press.

———. (1969). *Political Thinking and Consciousness*. Chicago: Markham.

Lane, R. (1973). *Political Man: Toward a Conceptual Base*. Beverly Hills, Calif: Sage.

Lao, R. C. (1970). Internal-external control and competent and innovative behavior among Negro college students. *Journal of Personality and Social Psychology, 14*, 263–270.

Lasswell, H. D. (1930). *Psychopathology and Politics*. Chicago: University of Chicago Press.

———. (1948). *World Politics and Personal Insecurity*. New York: Free Press.

———. (1965). *Power and Personality*. New York: Free Press.

Lefcourt, H. M. (1965). Risk-taking in Negro and white adults. *Journal of Personality and Social Psychology, 2*, 765–770.

———. (1966). Internal vs. external control of reinforcements. *Psychological Bulletin, 65*, 206–220.

———. (1972). Recent Developments in the Study of Locus of Control. In Maher, B. A. (Ed.). *Progress in Experimental Personality Research*. New York: Academic Press.

———. (1976). *Locus of Control*. New York: Academic Press.

Leites, N. (1953). *A Study in Bolshevism*. New York: Free Press.

Lenin, N. (1969). *What is to Be Done?* New York: Free Press.

Levinson, H. (1980). Criteria for choosing chief executives. *Harvard Business Review*, July/August, 113–119.

Lewis, W. A. (1955). *Theory of Economic Growth*. London: Allen & Unwin.

Likert, R. (1974). An Emerging Theory of Organization, Leadership and Management. In Tedeschi, J. (Ed.). *Perspectives on Social Power*. Chicago: Aldine.

Lippmann, W. (1965). *Public Opinion*. New York: Free Press.

Maccoby, M. (1976). *The Gamesman*. New York: Simon & Schuster.

MacDonald, A. P., Jr. (1971). Internal-external locus of control: parental antecedents. *Journal of Consulting and Clinical Psychology, 37*, 141–147.

———. (1973). Internal-External Locus of Control. In Robinson, J. P., and Shaver, P. R. (Eds.). *Measures of Social-Psychological Attitudes*. Ann Arbor, Mich.: Institute for Social Research.

Machiavelli, N. (1971). *The Prince and Selected Discourses*. New York: Bantam Books.

Mann, R. D. (1959) A review of the relationship between personality and performance in small groups. *Psychology Bulletin, 56*, 241–270.

Mannheim, K. (1936). *Ideology and Utopia*. New York: Harcourt, Brace and World.

Margiotta, F. (1979). A Military Elite in Transition: Air Force Leaders in the 1980's. Unpublished Ph.D thesis, Cambridge, Mass.: MIT.

Maroldo, G. K., and Flachmeier, L. C. (1978). Machiavellianism, locus of control, and cognitive style of American and West German coeds. *Psychological Reports, 42*, 1315–1317.

Maslow, A. (1973). Deficiency Motivation and Growth Motivation. In McClelland, D. C., and Steele, R. S. (Eds.). *Human Motivation: A Book of Readings*. Morristown, N.J.: General Learning Press.

May, R. (1977). *The Meaning of Anxiety*. New York: Norton.

Mazlish, B. (1976). *The Revolutionary Ascetic*. New York: Basic Books.

McClelland, D. C. (1961). *The Achieving Society*. New York: Free Press.

———. (1976). *Power: The Inner Experience*. Irvington, N.J.: Halstead Press.

———, and Winter, D. G. (1969). *Motivating Economic Achievement*. New York: Free Press.

McClelland, D. C., and Burnham, D. (1976). Power is the great motivator. *Harvard Business Review*, March-April, 110–111.

McClelland, D. C., and Steele, R. S. (1972). *Human Motivation Workshops. A Book of Readings*. Morristown, N.J.: General Learning Press.

McClelland, D. C., et al. (1972). *The Drinking Man*. New York: Free Press.

McGhee, P.E., and Crandall, V. C. (1968). Beliefs in internal-external control of reinforcements and academic performance. *Child Development, 39*, 92–102.

Merton, R. K. (1965). Bureaucratic Structure and Personality. In Gouldner, A. W. (Ed.). *Studies in Leadership*. New York: Russell and Russell.

——— (1968). *Social Theory and Social Structure*. New York: Free Press.

Messer, S. B. (1972). The relationship of internal-external locus of control to academic performance. *Child Development, 43*, 1456–1462.

Milbrath, L. W., and Klein, W. (1962). Personality correlates of political partici-pation. *Acta Sociologica, 6*, 53–66.

Mirels, H. E. (1970). Dimensions of internal vs. external locus of control. *Journal of Consulting and Clinical Psychology, 34*, 226–228.

Moore, W. E. (1969). Climbers, Riders and Treaders. In Rosen, D. C. (Ed.). *Achievement in American Society*, Cambridge, Mass.: Schenkman.

Mosca, G. (1939). *The Ruling Class*. New York: McGraw-Hill.

Mullahay, P. (1968). *Psychoanalysis and Interpersonal Psychiatry: The Contributions of Harry Stack Sullivan*. New York: Science House.

Murphy, G. (1966). *Personality: A Biosocial Approach to Origins and Structure*. New York: Basic Books.

Pareto, V. (1935). *Mind and Society*. New York: Harcourt, Brace.

Parsons, T. (1964). *Social Theory and Social Structure*. Glencoe, Ill: Free Press.

Presthus, R. (1962). *The Organizational Society*. New York: Vintage Books.

Pye, L. W. (1976). *Mao Tse Tung: The Man in the Leader*. New York: Basic Books.

Randle, C. W. (1956). How to identify promotable executives. *Harvard Business Review*, May-June, 122–134.

Reid, D. W., and Ware, E. (1973). Multidimensionality of internal-external locus of control: implications for past and future research. *Canadian Journal of Behavioral Science, 5*, 264–271.

Riesman, D. (1950). *The Lonely Crowd*. New Haven, Conn.: Yale University Press.

Riker, W. (1974). The Nature of Trust. In Tedeschi, J. (Ed.). *Perspectives on Social Power*. Chicago: Aldine.

Robinson, J. P., and Shaver P. R. (1973). *Measures of Social-Psychological Attitudes*. Ann Arbor, Mich.: Institute for Social Research.

Rokeach, M. (1960). *The Open and Closed Mind*. New York: Basic Books.

Rosenberg, M. (1965). *Society and the Adolescent Self-Image*. Princeton, N.J.: Princeton University Press.

Rothberg, D. L. (1980). Professional achievement and locus of control: a tenuous inference reconsidered. *Psychological Reports, 46*, 184–188.

Rotter, J. C. (1966). Generalized expectancies for internal vs. external control of reinforcements. *Psychological Monographs, 80* (Whole No. 609).

Ryckman, R. M., and Sherman, M. F. (1972). Interactive effects of locus of control and sex of subject on confidence ratings and performance in achievement-related situations. Paper presented to the American Psychological Association, Hawaii.

Schein, E. H. (1978). *Career Dynamics: Matching Individual and Organizational Needs.* Reading, Mass.: Addison-Wesley.

Schumpeter, J. (1934). *The Theory of Economic Development.* Cambridge, Mass.: Harvard University Press.

———. (1962). *Capitalism, Socialism and Democracy.* Cambridge, Mass.: Harvard University Press.

Shiply, T. E., and Veroff, J. (1952). A projective measure of the need for affiliation. *Journal of Experimental Psychology, 43,* 349–356.

Simon, H. (1957). *Administrative Behavior.* New York: Free Press.

Smith, M. B. (1968). A map for the analysis of personality and politics. *Journal of Social Issues, 24,* 15–28.

Spranger, E. (1966). *Types of Men: Psychology and Ethics of Personality.* New York: Johnson Reprint Corporation.

Stodgill, R. M. (1974). *Handbook of Leadership.* New York: Free Press.

Sullivan, H. S. (1953). *The Interpersonal Theory of Psychiatry.* New York: Norton.

Tawney, R. (1926). *Religion and the Rise of Capitalism.* New York: Harcourt, Brace.

Tedeschi, J. (Ed.). (1974). *Perspectives on Social Power.* Chicago: Aldine.

Thayer, R. E. (1967). Measurement of activation through self-report. *Psychological Reports, 20,* 663–678.

Troeltsch, E. (1912). *Protestantism and Progress.* London: Allen & Unwin.

Veroff, J., and Feld, S. (1970). *Marriage and Work in America.* New York: Van Nostrand Reinhold.

Wallace, A. F. (1956). Stress and rapid personality changes. *International Record of Medicine, 169,* 761–764.

Watson, D. (1967). Relationship between locus of control and anxiety. *Journal of Personality and Social Psychology*, 6, 91–92.

Weber, M. (1949). *Methodology for the Social Sciences*. New York: Free Press.

———. (1958). *The Protestant Ethic and the Spirit of Capitalism*. New York: Scribners.

Wells, L. E., and Marwell, G. (1976). *Self-Esteem: Its Conceptualization and Measurement*. Beverly Hills, Calif: Sage.

Whyte, W. H. (1956). *The Organization Man*. New York: Simon & Schuster.

Wildavsky, A. (1980). Review of *Changing of the Guard: Power and Leadership in America*, by David S. Broder. *New York Times Review of Books*, August 31.

Winter, D. G. (1973). *The Power Motive*. New York: Free Press.

Wittgenstein, L. (1945). *Philosophical Investigations*. New York: MacMillan.

Wylie, R. (1961). *The Self-Concept*. Lincoln, Neb.: University of Nebraska Press.

Zalesnik, A., and De Vries, MFR (1975). *Power and the Corporate Mind*. Boston: Houghton Mifflin.

———. (1977). Leaders and managers: are they different? *Harvard Business Review*, May-June, 67–78.

Ziller, R., et al. (1969). Self-esteem: a self-social construct. *Journal of Consulting and Clinical Psychology*, 33, 85–95.

AUTHOR INDEX

SUBJECT INDEX

209

ABOUT THE AUTHOR

David Rothberg received his Ph.D. in political science from the Massachusetts Institute of Technology, where he studied political psychology and organizational behavior. His professional experience includes public opinion polling and policy research and consulting in the health care sector. Dr. Rothberg has taught at American University, Tufts University, and at MIT and has published several articles and book reviews in political science, psychology, and health care journals. His first book, *Regional Variations in Hospital Use: Geographic and Temporal Patterns of Care in the United States*, was published in 1981.

Dr. Rothberg is currently a human resources consultant for Prime Computer, Inc., of Natick Massachusetts.